SOUVENIR OF
THE OPENING
OF THE
EDINBURGH
BALMORAL HOTEL

FIRST PUBLISHED 1902
REPUBLISHED 1991 WITH NEW
CHAPTER BY FAY YOUNG,
ILLUSTRATIONS BY KATE ISLES

PUBLISHED BY INSIDER PUBLICATIONS LIMITED, EDINBURGH
PRINTED BY B.A.S. PRINTERS LIMITED, OVER WALLOP, HAMPSHIRE
BOUND BY HUNTER & FOULIS LIMITED, EDINBURGH

ISBN 1 8710570 8 6

LIST OF ILLUSTRATIONS.

MARY, QUEEN OF SCOTS

Edinburgh Castle and Nor' Loch

OLD AND NEW EDINBURGH.

HE stranger from the South in former times approached Edinburgh by slow stages, and entered it with wary circumspection, often in fear and trembling; he could reckon neither on welcome nor entertainment. Long after the Union of the Crowns and the Civil War, he met with challenge and impost at the city gates and ran the gauntlet of sour and suspicious looks from the citizens. Colonel Mannering and Dr Samuel Johnson complained in the eighteenth century, as Froissart had done in the fourteenth and Brantôme in the sixteenth, of niggardly fare, sluttish service, and straitened accommodation. Then, as now, Edinburgh was a town of memories, beautiful for situation, filled with the spirit and bodying forth the form of romance. But it was long also the town of broil and feud, of narrow thoroughfares and prejudices, of evil smells and customs.

"We have changed all that." From the corridor carriage of a London express, one can smile at the pride with which worthy Mr Jedediah Cleishbotham congratulated the readers of the "Heart of Midlothian," seventy or eighty years ago, on the headlong speed of the mail-coach of the day, as it "rolled its thunder" through Gandercleuch or round the base of Arthur Seat, compared with the slow pace of the "miserable horse-cart" which, thirty years before, carried news and passengers to the Scottish capital at the rate of thirty miles per diem; and, in a Princes Street hotel, one is well placed for pitying the case of poor Miss Winnifred Jenkins as the guest of an "ordinary" in the Canongate.

The new-time traveller to Edinburgh, having skirted the famous hill which seems to guard, like a crouching lion, the grey palace of Holyrood at its feet, plunges through the Calton tunnel to emerge in the depths of the hollow between Old and

New Edinburgh. He feels as if some magician's wand had smitten the rock, and opened the way into the heart of an enchanted city. On the one hand, the houses of "Auld Reekie" rise high and higher as they climb the steep ridge from the Abbey to the Castle, until they seem to beetle, like tall fantastic cliffs, over the head of the traveller; on the other, from a not less noble vantage-ground of rock and slope, shine the towers and pillars and fair palace fronts of "Modern Athens."

Nature and art, beauty and utility, the venerable and the modern, are found in strange and not inharmonious conjunction in this "Valley of the Winds," where the North British Railway has planted its head-quarters. Green banks and braes, wooded lawns and parterres of flowers divide the space with platforms and signal-boxes; the living rock rises from the very margin of the railway track. The visitor finds himself at the root and foundation of the old city as well as in the centre of its modern life. He can peruse its historic and prehistoric records written on its stones, or plunge into the current of its present-day fashion and traffic without stirring far from the spot where his train has set him down. The Nor' Loch— Edinburgh's old moat of defence, originally formed to keep the Southerner at a respectful distance—has been drained in order that he may have easy entrance and exit. Trains move out and in, and children play, where the citizens of earlier generations boated and fished, and drowned witches and malefactors. A channel has been made for commerce under the Earthen Mound—the mound of shot rubbish of Old Edinburgh—by which, and by the North Bridge, it first stepped across the valley to take possession of the site of the New Town. The intrusive railway brushes the base of the Castle rock and burrows below the West Kirk churchyard on its way to Glasgow and to the Forth Bridge.

Many momentous changes in the fortunes and in the aspect of the city have been brought about by the choice of the trough between Old and New Edinburgh as the main channel of the railway traffic. Other old landmarks besides the Nor' Loch have suffered obliteration through coming in the ruthless path of the engineer and the innovator. One may look in vain for the site of the Pilgrim Well of St Triduana, virgin and martyr, now lost in the maze of engine-repairing sheds at St Margaret's; and, buried under the rails and platforms of Waverley Station, is the ground on which once stood the Trinity College Church and Hospital, the princely foundation of Mary of Gueldres, Queen of James II. of Scots, although the Church has been in part re-erected in the neighbouring Jeffrey Street. Other things, good and evil, the "river of human life" that rushes to-day through the old "Dead Sea" of the Nor' Loch has swept away in its impetuous course; and, as has been written, the focus of its forces is under and around the arches of the North Bridge:—

"Here, converging currents, from south and north, and from east and west, meet and jostle; and there are times and seasons when travelling and holiday-making humanity swells in an autumn flood and seethes and eddies about the piers and abutments. Under stress of this irresistible movement, older structures are

8

continually being undermined and toppling down. The Waverley Station is the centre of a dissolving view of city alterations. Looking down upon it, you behold a furrowed and spreading 'sea of glass,' from which escape the smoke and the shriek of the toiling locomotives; and bounding it, ancient walls that crumble to their ruin, and new walls that climb the sky in their place; while at night, when you carry your eye away from the brilliant constellation of the New Town lamps and the dimmer but more impressive galaxy that irradiates the dark mass of the Old Town, the gulf below is seen to be filled with many-coloured lights, both fixed and moving."

From the windows of the new North British Station Hotel, the eye commands this wonderful spectacle as from no other view-point of the city; and its great Clock Tower may be reckoned as among the chief of Edinburgh's "high places." It overtops the loftiest of the High Street "lands," and all but a few of the spires of the New Town; it raises the spectator to the level of the floor of the Castle Rock, of the summit of the Calton Hill Monuments, and of the loftiest turn of the Radical Road; and it is placed at the very "centre of gravity" of the city's business and population—at the confluence of New Town and Old Town traffic. As from Teufelsdröckh's window, you gaze down upon the floods of humanity flowing from, and towards, the four winds of heaven, and study the whole life-circulation of the city, Princes Street, "the finest promenade in Europe," is enfiladed from end to end, and the broad current of its carriages and passengers meets at the base of your watch-tower—between it and its next neighbours, the General Register House and the General Post Office—the more motley crowds that pour through the widened channel of the North Bridge, that surge up by Leith Street from the once vassal port of Leith, or that stream in more thinly by Waterloo Place, from the direction of Edinburgh's new coast territory of Portobello.

Or, looking around and abroad, you can survey a scene the like of which is not to be found in any other land or city; and at the same time lay plans for exploring in detail the enchanted ground of Old and New Edinburgh. The "City Beautiful" lies below, in the length thereof and the breadth thereof, spread out as on a map. One by one, you can note its landmarks and consider its palaces; look down into the profound depths of its hollows, filled with smoke or with greenery, or count its heights, crowned with pillars, spires, and turrets. From the "draughty parallelograms"—the stately but somewhat too regular array of squares and terraces—that cover the Northern slopes, you turn to the "ridgy back" which the Old Town still heaves to the sky. Time and "city improvement" may have despoiled it of features which one would fain have kept. But they have added others which preserve the bold irregularity of outline which is one of the chief notes and charms of Old Edinburgh; the new "Scotsman" buildings—the *vis-à-vis* of the Station Hotel across the valley—and other recent additions to the Old Town architecture make a foreground not unworthy even of the mural crown of St Giles and the majestic mass of the Castle.

VIEW FROM TOWER OF NORTH BRITISH STATION HOTEL—LOOKING WEST

VIEW FROM TOWER OF NORTH BRITISH STATION HOTEL—LOOKING NORTH-EAST

Castle
from
Grassmarket

From our watch-tower we can see, also, out and away over even the lofty *chevaux-de-frise* of the High Street chimneys and pinnacles, to the outlines of the Pentlands and the Lammermoors — ground made sacred by the genius of Sir Walter Scott and of R. L. Stevenson. Nearer at hand, Arthur Seat and its crags, those haunts of a hundred legends and traditions, stand fair and full in view; and "the gallant Firth the eye may note," from the Bass and the May to the Forth Bridge, and far beyond; the profile, to sky and sea, of the whole "Kingdom of Fife"; and in dimmer distance still other and greater kingdoms of Scottish history and romance—the peaks and recesses of the Highlands.

To the grand old Castle on its rock the roving eye returns, as to a magnet, from the survey of this glorious prospect. From whatever side our City is viewed, it fills a large part of the horizon—it crowns the scene. This "Rock of Observation," as some would interpret its old Celtic name of *Mynedh Agnedh*, was the foundation stone on which the town was built. Its shape looms up out of the mists of the past, vague but impressive, as the great Rock and its battlements loom to-day when the "haar" out of the North Sea chokes the valley below. The "Castle of the Maidens," the "Castle Inviolate," are other titles by which it is known in the chronicles; there is no spot more consecrated to the romance of history, to the faithful championship of the lost or the desperate cause. It still guards—as if they were symbols of its past—the Regalia of the Kingdom; the earliest Scottish house of prayer still covered by a roof; the most famous and ponderous specimen of our ancient ordnance; the first hall of meeting of the nation's parliaments, and the prison-house of the noblest of its prisoners of state. On Edinburgh Rock the "Union" was born, in the person of James I. and VI.; and from it was fired the last shot in the long and bloody quarrel between the kingdoms.

Even the "through-passenger" can spy a little of the Story of the Rock as he flashes past, almost under, its frowning cliffs. If he knows when and where to look, he can glimpse the postern gate, or "sallyport," through which the wasted

EDINBURGH CASTLE
FROM ESPLANADE

corpse of Margaret, saint and queen, was smuggled secretly by night, for sepulture in Dunfermline; and to which, many stormy centuries later, "Bonnie Dundee" clambered to hold talk with "the Gordon," captain of the Castle, before riding to Killiecrankie and death. Visible, too, are the precipitous way by which Randolph escaladed the Rock in the War of Independence, and the tower built in David the Saint's "garden of herbs" on the margin of the Nor' Loch, whence the garrison drew part of their precarious water supply. But in these days there are easy and peaceful means of ingress by the Esplanade, over the drawbridge of the empty moat, and through the open Portcullis Gate, to the highest summit, the oldest and innermost sanctuary, of "High Dunedin."

Perhaps the buildings are not wholly worthy of the site and its associations. They have been much patched, and there has not been time for recent restorations and additions to compose in tone with the smoky-grey of the older portions.

Banqueting Hall, Castle

The visitor who brings hither exalted notions of regal and priestly state in the heroic and feudal ages, may be disappointed by the tiny proportions of St Margaret's Chapel, and by the shabby air of the Royal Apartments in which Mary passed some memorable weeks in the interval between Rizzio's slaughter and Darnley's murder. But there can be no disappointment with the renowned and marvellous view from the King's Bastion, at the muzzle of "Roaring Meg" of Mons, silent since she burst in firing a salute in honour of the last, and worst, of the Stuart Kings; or with the peep from the bedroom window through which the "Modern Solomon" first saw the light of day, into the abyss of the Grassmarket lying at the foot of that sheer cliff, over which another royal infant, his great-great-grandfather "James with the Fiery Face," was "towed in a blanket," to be taken to a place of greater safety at Stirling.

Memories, from the days of Canmore and Bruce to those of Walter Scott, crowd the mean chamber where the ancient "Honours of Scotland" are "hidden for exposure"; they haunt also the renovated Argyll or Constable Tower—the State Prison, where "the Great Marquis" of Argyll and his foe, "the Great Marquis" of Montrose (their bones now rest in opposite aisles of St Giles' Church) slept their last sleep on earth. Filled with these ghosts of the past, too, is the

Banqueting Hall, now nobly restored as an Armoury, whence the young heirs of the House of Douglas were savagely dragged from the feast to execution in the courtyard outside; and the Vaults beneath reckon James Mhor Macgregor and the Vicomte Anne de St Ives among their shadowy inhabitants.

But we must not, in a bird's-eye survey of Edinburgh, dally over these annals and legends of the city's oldest "Mount of Vision." It has been said of Prague that every stone is a morsel of history. As much might be said of Edinburgh Castle, and indeed of the Old Town from the Rock to the Palace. In the incomparable thoroughfare which, bearing different names, runs, for more than a mile, down the long slope from the Castle Esplanade to the precincts of Holyrood, the heart of Old Edinburgh beat for many centuries, and still beats. It has seen and suffered great changes, notably in recent years; but it has not wholly lost the aspect and character that drew wondering and admiring remarks from the visitor to the High Street, the Canongate and the Lawnmarket in the age of the Stuarts and of the early Georges. Of the ground on which it stands, it can still be written that "it carries more houses and population, and perhaps more history and romance than any corresponding area in Europe." For long it was the very "cockpit of the kingdom," the stage on which a large part of a tumultuous and bloody national drama was enacted. Rival sects and factions fought out their quarrels at the Netherbow or on "the rigging of the Hie Gait," and Border thief and Highland chieftain brought their clan feuds and family vendettas here for settlement. From the innumerable narrow side passages of wynd and close, issued the characters in the tragedy and comedy of Old Edinburgh street life in sudden sally or surprise, and withdrew again in triumph or in precipitate retreat; and every close had, and still has, its own rich store of history and tradition.

Times have been known when Edinburgh waged savage war, not only with the neighbour burgh of Leith, but with the adjacent "court suburb" of Canongate, the prolongation of its principal street; and when the city bombarded the Castle, and the Castle sent back hot answer into the heart of the closes. Among the pictures of the past are included such scenes as the gathering of the citizens round the "Mercat Croce," at "the jow of the common bell," to hear the dread news from Flodden; John Knox speaking to the multitude from the window of his house which still juts out into the High Street near the Netherbow; Bothwell and his accomplices meeting Mary and her flambeau-bearers in the Blackfriars' Wynd, as she took her way back to Holyrood from the doomed house at Kirk o' Field; Montrose going proudly to execution; Prince Charlie, with no foreboding of Culloden in his heart, riding gaily to take possession of the Palace of his fore-fathers, and the fierce Edinburgh mob rushing through the streets to "drown" the image of their patron, Saint Giles, to burn the Chapel Royal, or to take vengeance on the signatories of the "woeful Union," or on Jock Porteous.

A host of other memories cling to the "plainstanes" or linger in the closes

of the High Street and the Canongate. One is reminded, by a name, or a fragment of corbelling, inscription, or armorial bearing, of some famous resident or guest of the old city, some literary association, some character or incident in Scott's novels. The whole scene is indeed pervaded by the spirit of Waverley romance. It divides possession with the spirit of history. One looks almost more keenly, in the region of the West Bow and the Lawnmarket, for the spot where Bartoline Saddletree's shop might have stood, "at the head of Bess Wynd," than for the door through which the nefarious Deacon Brodie fared forth in his midnight excursions; Roland Græme's quarters at "My Lord Setoun's ludging" take our fancy above the hiding-place where Chiesley of Dalry lay in wait to shoot Lord-President Lockhart, or the site of the house of that Old Edinburgh bogey, Major Weir himself. Peter Peebles is more an inhabiting spirit of Parliament Close than Knox, who lies buried below its stones, or any of the great crowd of "heroes and martyrs" who have perished under the public eye beneath the shadow of St Giles. It is chiefly remembrance of the Waverley suppers at Jamie Ballantyne's that makes us turn under the archway into St John Street, although here lived the eccentric Monboddo and his daughter, the "fair Burnet"; here Burns was initiated into the "mystic tie," and here Tobias Smollett wrote part of his "Humphrey Clinker"; and sympathy with the fate of Fergus M'Ivor, as much as interest in the quaint house architecture of a former day, guides our steps into the White Horse Close.

It was the peculiar fortune of Edinburgh that, after it had ceased to be the seat of a Court and the meeting-place of a Parliament, it became a capital of letters; to its feudal age succeeded its literary age. Peace came, and, with it, progress in all the arts of life. But still, for generations, the old city abode within the narrow bounds fixed by the needs and circumstances of an earlier day; it only crowded its houses more closely upon its ridge, and added more storeys to its lofty "lands." Fashion went in sedan chairs—for there was small space for wheeled carriages—to rout or ball in the Assembly Rooms at the West Bow or in the Old Assembly Close, or tiptoed through the mire to St Cecilia's Hall in Niddry's Wynd—at the corner of the Cowgate—to listen to Tenducci's singing, or to the latest composition of Mozart or Handel. Lords and lairds, learned divines and men of science, judges profound in the law and renowned in letters, were, with their families, "pigeon-holed in narrow chambers, up many flights of stairs, in some tall tenement, where they could shake hands with their neighbours on the other side of the close." There were "howffs" where they turned in regularly for their morning potations; they "took the air" on the Castlehill, in the "Duke's Walk" of the King's Park, or by the margin of the Burgh Loch; those who had literary inclinations dropped into the library of Allan Ramsay, the periwig-maker, or, in a later day, into Creech's shop in the Luckenbooths or Archibald Constable's musty premises above the Netherbow. Even the womankind among "the persons of quality" did not disdain to sup socially and frugally in chop-house or oyster-cellar; and, at night, the male portion of Old Edinburgh society, in its several classes and degrees, found its way to its convivial clubs and taverns in Fleshmarket Close, Writers' Court, and less select quarters, and gave its mind and time seriously to hard drinking until the "sma' hours."

Truly, as has been said, "the beggar's toe galled the noble's kibes in Auld Reekie Hie Street! Poverty and riches elbowed each other on the pavement, and entered and issued from the same close-head. Long after the Court had forsaken the city, and after the clash of arms had ceased to be heard on the causeway, saint and sinner, gentle and simple, dwelt amicably together; and a section of one of the High Street tenements in the eighteenth century would have shown a section of society from top to bottom, arranged in regular strata, touching each other, yet never mixing. The humble tradesman lived on the ground floor or in the cellar, while the lord of Session or the dame of quality mounted to the fourth or fifth storey."

The "cream" of Edinburgh society has, long ago, been drained away from the neighbourhood of the High Street. The opening of the first North Bridge was the prelude of changes, in the social structure and in the appearance of the Old Town, which are still in progress. There are large and growing spaces, where not even a trace of the former life and architecture is left to prompt the imagination or fix any reminiscences of the past. The site of Mary of Guise's Palace, on the Castlehill, is occupied by the United Free Assembly Hall; and that of the Duke of Gordon's house opposite, by a Board School. Gone from its post is the quaint and venerable structure that long leaned over the Lawnmarket at the head of the West Bow. City improvements have swept away as effectively the congeries of narrow closes between Parliament Square and the Tron Kirk as did city fires their neighbours to the west; and the working-class dwellings that have taken their place hardly console the antiquary and the artist for the loss of a bit of Edinburgh history in stone. On the other side of the thoroughfare, the enlargement of the Council Chambers has made an end of the "Clerihugh's Tavern" of "Guy Mannering," and of other memorials of the past in Writers' Court and Warriston Close; and, in forming the magnificent structures that line the new North Bridge, sacrifice had to be made, on one side of the way, of Milne Square, with its traditions of Lovat, Neil Gow, and the Treaty of Union, and, on the other, of Robert Fergusson's birthplace in the old Cap-and-Feather Close, and of Allan Ramsay's timber-fronted shop "at the sign of the Mercury, opposite Niddry's Wynd."

In the Canongate and in the Abbey precincts also, the ploughshare of time and change has been busy among the old houses, and many ancient landmarks have been removed into the dustbin. New Street, where dwelt Lord Kames and Lord Hailes, is itself a thing of the past. But the fine sixteenth century Tolbooth of the Abbot's

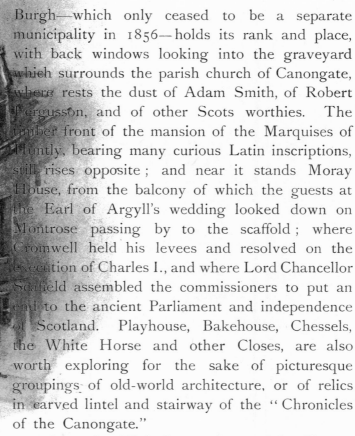

The Tolbooth

Burgh—which only ceased to be a separate municipality in 1856—holds its rank and place, with back windows looking into the graveyard which surrounds the parish church of Canongate, where rests the dust of Adam Smith, of Robert Fergusson, and of other Scots worthies. The timber front of the mansion of the Marquises of Huntly, bearing many curious Latin inscriptions, still rises opposite; and near it stands Moray House, from the balcony of which the guests at the Earl of Argyll's wedding looked down on Montrose passing by to the scaffold; where Cromwell held his levees and resolved on the execution of Charles I., and where Lord Chancellor Seafield assembled the commissioners to put an end to the ancient Parliament and independence of Scotland. Playhouse, Bakehouse, Chessels, the White Horse and other Closes, are also worth exploring for the sake of picturesque groupings of old-world architecture, or of relics in carved lintel and stairway of the "Chronicles of the Canongate."

To one who glances either up or down the High Street vista, "John Knox's House," at the Netherbow, with its gables, crowsteps, and outer stairs, its panelled rooms and dark nooks and corners, its pious mottoes and its many legends, is a "bit of old Edinburgh" that takes the eye and lingers in the memory. Its former rival, Adam Fullarton's House, may still be discovered on the other side of the way; the sculptured arms of the Abbot of Melrose can be seen over the entrance of his old "ludging" in Strichen's Close; in Advocates' Close and other uninviting entries from the High Street, also, sixteenth and seventeenth century dates, the heraldic bearings of noble and ancient families, and devout inscriptions, scarcely borne out by the history of the builders, can be discovered and perused; and, from the foot of Byres' Close, you can gaze up at the carved dormers, looking out upon the Firth, of the dwelling of that Adam Bothwell, Bishop of Orkney, whose worst day's work was to marry his kinsman, James Hepburn, to the Queen of Scots, and where afterwards lived the unhappy Lady Anne Bothwell of the ballad, who sang—

> Now Arthur Seat shall be my bed,
>   The sheets shall ne'er be pressed by me;
> St Anton's Well shall be my drink,
>   Since my false love's forsaken me.

Mercat
Cross

Though, with the rising of the New County Buildings has disappeared the last trace of Libberton's Wynd, at the head of which Burke of the "West Port murders," and many a notorious criminal besides, have been executed, the Lawnmarket continues to possess, in excellent preservation, its Riddle's Close; and here are chambers in which King Jamie and his Queen, Anne of Denmark, were feasted by the Magistrates, and David Hume wrote his great history and entertained his friends. Across the street, around the open space into which James Court and other Lawnmarket passages lead, one finds, along with buildings which have associations with Burns, with Hume, with Johnson and Boswell, and with Sir Walter Scott, the town mansion, built nearly three centuries ago and lately restored by Lord Rosebery, in which a Countess of Stair once "led Edinburgh fashion on the second flat of a common stair in a narrow Old Town close." Near by, another example is given of how the old may be preserved in the midst of the new, in the picturesque group of Ramsay Lodge, the core of which is the villa of the author of the "Gentle Shepherd," set on the edge of the Castle Braes, overlooking the railway and the New Town.

The "obstructions" in the fairway of Old Edinburgh traffic, which the townsfolk loved even while they grumbled at them, have, for the most part, gone the way of all the earth. The Luckenbooths and the Tolbooth—the "Heart of Midlothian"—disappeared wellnigh a century ago; the Netherbow, Edinburgh's Temple Bar, still earlier. The Salt Tron and the City Guard House, where that famous body, the "Town Rats," kept watch with halberds and Lochaber axes over the order and peace of the burgh, is a mere memory, like the "black banditti" themselves. But some of the Old Town fore-stairs still project into the pavement; some of the wells, behind which the water-caddies once stood in long *queue*, keep their guard in the High Street. The Mercat Croce—the centre of so many tragic and joyous spectacles—has been raised aloft on a new pedestal by the late Mr Gladstone.

Above all, the "Hie Kirk of St Giles" holds its place—may it always hold it! —on the "crown of the causey." After the Castle and the Abbey—if it comes after —it is the most venerable of the monuments of Old Edinburgh, although little more than foundations are left of the twelfth century church which, with the town itself, was burned down during an English raid in 1385. It was a cathedral only during the sixty years of much interrupted Episcopal predominance, between the flinging of Jenny Geddes's stool and the Revolution of 1689. But it has always been the "Town's Kirk." Its Gothic crown is one of the most beautiful and far-seen of the ornaments of Old Edinburgh. "Within and without, the fabric bears the scars, honourable or otherwise, of the tumults, invasions, civil wars and conflagrations of the past. Legend and history cling to its walls. It has been put to base as well as noble uses. Councils of barons and prelates have met in it in time of national danger; it has given shelter to the Estates of the Realm and to the High Court of Justice; it is the traditional scene of the weird High Mass celebrated on the eve of Flodden. Knox thundered in the Hie Kirk against the idolatries of Rome and the 'monstrous regimen of women.' When his voice grew too weak to be heard in the

Choir, he 'dang the pulpit to blads' in the adjoining and more restricted space of the Tolbooth Church, forming the southern side of St Giles." For among the other forms of desecration to which the edifice had to submit, it was divided up, until recent years, into several minor places of worship. It has received worthy restoration; and one can now wander within the walls, visit the Albany and Preston aisles; muse over the monuments of Moray, Argyll, and Montrose; study—near the reputed spot whence the three-legged stool of the kail-wife sang past the Dean's "lug"—the service books of the successive sects that have held sway in St Giles; look up at the tattered flags of the old Scots regiments that hang from arch and pillar, and acknowledge that the High Church may still lay claim to be the centre of the nation's religious life, and that its atmosphere breathes "lessons of unity and forbearance, rather than of the strife and divisions of old."

One cannot visit St Giles without also glancing into the neighbouring Parliament House; for here a different and yet kindred spirit dwells. It is the head and shrine of Scottish law. Under the noble oaken roof of the "Parliament Lobby" the Estates of the kingdom once sat framing statutes and dispensing justice. The "Laigh Parliament Hall" below—now occupied by the Advocates' Library— was the Star Chamber in which the Privy Council examined and, it is said, tortured prisoners in the "Killing Time." The faces of eminent judges and brilliant advocates look down from the walls of the Great Hall; one can fancy their ghosts—in company with the ghosts of their clients—haunting the place where they pleaded or decided causes and cracked their jokes. And kindliest and most familiar of all the Parliament House shades, is that of Sir Walter.

The back windows of this temple of the law look down into the murky depths of the Cowgate. The aspect of this debased thoroughfare, once a beautiful rural lane, then a residence of prelates and nobles, and now given over for the most part to the poorest of the poor, is a grim satire on the changes of custom and fashion. There is nothing left of Beaton's Palace, or of the Mint, or of other relics of "better days"; and what architecture it boasts is that of buildings, like the Carnegie Free Library, that rise out of it into streets that are in all senses higher up in the world than the lowly Cowgate. In a wynd leading out of it, Scott was born; another conducts to the "High School Yards," where the future author of "Waverley" made a brighter figure than in the class; and at its western end, the Cowgate opens into the historic Grassmarket.

Here, under the Castle Rock, between the Bowfoot and the West Port, there are names and objects reminiscent of the days when the eyes and the heart of the nation were turned towards the gallow's foot. A cross marks, on the paving-stones, the site of the scaffold where so many sufferers for conscience sake "glorified God in the Grassmarket"; beside it, Captain Porteous was hung from a dyer's pole, by the mob of 1736. In or near this ancient and spacious market-place—the point of arrival and departure of Edinburgh's visitors for many centuries—were transacted other momentous scenes in the drama of Scottish ecclesiastical and national history. In Magdalene Chapel, at the Cowgate-head— a *Maison Dieu*, founded before Flodden—met the General Assembly of 1578, which proclaimed the deposition of Episcopal rule in the Church; and in the same ancient building, the "National Covenant" of 1638 was prepared for signature on the "throch stones" of the adjoining Greyfriars' Churchyard, where afterwards some of the subscribers "sealed their testimony" with their blood.

Greyfriars is indeed "a very battlefield of old creeds and factions, strewn and heaped with the corpses of those who, while in life, hated each other to the death."

From the "Martyrs' Monument" you can stroll to that of their persecutor, the "Bluidy Mackenzie"; and, in the strangely mingled company of the sleepers, are George Buchanan and the Regent Morton, Allan Ramsay and "Pope Adam Gib" of the "Auld Lichts," Captain Porteous and the "Man of Feeling." In a corner of this grimmest and most interesting of Scottish "God's-acres," the long arm that stretches southward to what was once the Flodden Wall, the weary and despairing crowd of the Bothwell Brig prisoners were huddled for months, until they could be shipped off to the plantations; and, at the gate, after listening demurely in the Old Greyfriars to the sermon preached from the pulpit of Principal Robertson, young Scott held his umbrella, for a blissful minute, above the head of his "Lady Green Mantle," before their ways parted—for life. Love, as well as Death, knows something of the "Yairds of the Grey Freiris."

Scott's house was near by, in George Square—in those days a city suburb. It is outside the old Town Wall, part of which still bounds the grounds of Heriot's Hospital—"Jingling Geordie's" munificent gift, which has been for well nigh three centuries a blessing and an ornament to his native town. Other fragments of the Wall are to be seen at Bristo Port, and at the corner of Drummond Street and Pleasance. These defences enclosed the lands of the Black Friars and the Church of St Mary-in-the-Fields—that "Kirk o' Field" of fateful and mysterious memory, over whose site now rises the dome of "Our Townis College," crowned by the aspiring figure of "Golden Youth" bearing aloft the torch of knowledge. The black deeds and evil traditions of the past could not have had nobler redress than in the illustrious record of the University, whose own traditions now go back for more than three hundred years. It is girt about by other buildings—like the Museum of Science and Art—whose office it also is to spread abroad sweetness and light; and, like the Old Town itself, the Old Town's College has broken bounds and planted its new Medical School and M'Ewan Hall, alongside the new Royal Infirmary, close to George Square and to the borders of those Meadows that were once the bed of the Burgh Loch.

Far beyond the domes and towers and pinnacles of these temples of learning and healing, and the green interlude afforded by the trees and sward of the Meadows and Bruntsfield Links, stretches the city to the southward. Brown Square and St John's Hill, to which fashion, with a wrench like that of "divorcing soul from body," shifted from its closes for the sake of better air and more elbow room, have themselves become venerable and disappearing features of Old Edinburgh. Potterrow and Wester Portsburgh, once extra-mural villages with their own courts and corporations, have become overcrowded central slums and the scenes of the old or recent activities of the city improver, whose broom has cleared out of their place the house of Burns' "Clarinda" and the "murder hole" of Burke and Hare. The "tale of mean streets" of St Leonards and Crosscauseway is continued in the handsome suburb of Newington. The main artery of southward traffic, the

HOLYROOD PALACE

South Bridge, itself dating from 1785, stretches out for miles into what, in Sir Walter's time, was green and open country, to the foot and up the ascent of Liberton Hill.

"Villadom" has occupied and almost obliterated the site of "St Catherine's Convent in the Sciennes," and has surrounded, and threatens to annex, the fine old manor houses of the Grange and Bruntsfield. The south-flowing stream of suburban dwellings and population, has, in one direction, approached Craigmillar—

> "A chiefless castle, breathing soft farewells
> From stern but leafy walls, where ruin greenly dwells."

In another, the tide has closely girt about Merchiston Castle, also a "stronghold of Old Romance" and haunt of associations with Mary Stuart. It has submerged the ground, on the Burgh Muir, where, around the King's Standard on the Bore Stone, the Scottish host assembled for the march to Flodden; it has poured down the slope of Morningside and crossed the Burn of Braid; and it washes the feet and knees of the Blackford, the Braids, and the Craiglockhart Hills.

One of the hills that surrounds and looks down upon Edinburgh, still holds the city at arm's length. This is its chief hill of all—Arthur Seat—the guardian shape that, from the earliest dawn of its history, has kept watch and ward over its changing fortunes and its growing form. Dwelling houses, distilleries and gas-houses crowd up to the margin of this noblest and most picturesque of public parks; but no more than in the days when the braes of St Leonard's and Dumbiedykes were grazed by the sheep and kine of "douce Davie Deans" do they overpass its sacred precincts. The once "Innocent Railway" runs in between "Samson's Ribs" and the "Wells o' Wearie"; breweries and other noisome industries are occupying the fields of Prestonfield and of Duddingston, and pressing in upon the sheltered nook behind the hill where the tower of the ancient Norman church—in which Thomson, the landscape painter, preached—rises over the Loch with its sedges and its swans. But those who, after the example of "Reuben Butler" and Walter Scott, climb in the morning hours by the "wild path winding around the foot of the high belt of semi-circular rocks called Salisbury Crags," can be promised, along with the same sublime and ever-changing spectacle, only enriched with new features both of town and country, the same solitude. Or, if they choose to mount higher—by Muschet's Cairn and St Anthony's Well and Chapel, or by the Echoing Rock and Dunsappie Loch, to the Lion's Crown—there breaks upon the view a still more spacious, though it may be not a more impressive, prospect of land and sea, of the loveliness of nature and the wonders of art, than is to be seen even from the "Radical Road," or from the Clock Tower of the North British Station Hotel.

It is the Abbey and Palace below that have guarded the Hill from invasion and annexation. For the "King's Park" is part of the territory and sanctuary of Holyrood; and, from a wide circuit, we have worked our way back to the foot of the Canongate, and to the root of Old Edinburgh life and history. The Hill repays the gift it owes to the hoary "House of Kings"; for if, on one side, it is pressed upon by the squalor and noise of a poor city quarter, on the other it looks out and up "to the red crags and shadowed clefts of its great and quiet neighbour, Arthur Seat," which has varied little in face since David, the "Sair Saint," hunted the fabled "White Hart," and bestowed on his Monastery, planted on the spot, the sacred "Black Rood," which Edward I. afterwards carried across the Border along with the Coronation Stone of Scone.

The year 1128 is given as the date of the legendary event placed at the beginning of the annals of Holyrood. Much has happened since then. From a seat of Augustinian monks, Holyrood became a royal residence, the chief and favourite resort of the Scottish Court. The Palace appropriated the monastic buildings, and even infringed upon the Church; and then the Court deserted the old shell, as the Canons had done, and now, except for a few days in the year, when the shadow of royalty, in the form of the Lord High Commissioner, visits Edinburgh to open the General Assembly, the Picture Gallery of the Scottish Kings, like the roofless Chapel Royal, is abandoned to the tourist and the sightseer.

Such, in outline, is the history of Holyrood during seven or eight centuries. But that story has infinite and most startling details. The Abbey Church is a "beautiful wreck," comprehending all styles of Gothic, from the simple Norman lines of the earliest builders to the florid work expended on the doorway and west front of the Chapel Royal by Charles I. "James II. and VII." restored the Chapel for service, according to the Roman ritual, not long before the Revolution mob put their hands to the work of destruction done in previous generations by English raids and by civil wars. Under the floor of the Chapel, once the nave of the Abbey Church, rests the dust of many noble Scottish families; and here, too, are the tombs, put in decent repair by order of the Good Queen Victoria, of her royal predecessors, King David Bruce and James II. and James V. of Scots. The reputed graves of Rizzio and of Darnley are also pointed out in Holyrood Abbey Church, not far from the spot where, so few weeks after the Kirk o' Field explosion, the beautiful Queen of Scots gave her hand to Bothwell.

Long before the Court had "played the cuckoo" to the churchmen, the "Monastery of the Crag of Holyrood" had been the theatre of national events. It was the meeting place of parliaments and councils; Edward Baliol rendered homage in it to Edward III., and it gave hospitable entertainment to John of Gaunt. Fergus, the last of the semi-independent Pictish Lords of Galloway, came to Holyrood to pass his last days as a humble monk; and, in 1429, the semi-independent Lord of the Isles craved pardon here before James, the Poet

King, in his "shirt and drawers," for his crime of burning Inverness. There were great revels at the Abbey when James IV. brought hither his "English Rose," Margaret Tudor, and the marriage was celebrated which, later, brought about the Union of the Kingdoms. They were revels that ill accorded with the rules of a religious house; and James V. set in earnest about the work of pulling down the monastery and rearing a royal château in the prevailing style of the age, borrowed, like so many other things Scottish of that day, from France. The north-western wing of Holyrood is believed to contain part of the "fair palace, with three fair towers, to rest into when he was pleased to come," built, in 1525, by the father of Mary Stuart.

In it, he received his first lovely but fragile Queen, the "Lily of France." But it is with the fate of his daughter that the historic rooms of old Holyrood are chiefly associated. In these faded chambers, still hung with the old tapestries, the Queen of Scots danced and feasted, or passed hours of weeping and despair, listened to the lutings of Davie and of Chastelard, or to the harsh chidings of Knox—with all her faults a very woman, and a Queen with the spirit of a man. Her darkest hour was when the conspirators, led by her caitiff husband, stole, by the

secret staircase, into her little supping-room, and stabbed her faithful secretary in her presence; it was then that she put aside better thoughts and "studied revenge."

The "art treasures" of Holyrood, in pictures and old furniture, may be of no great value as art, except the fine fifteenth century diptyches in the gallery where Prince Charles Edward held his levees and balls; but they are precious as illustrations of closed pages of Scottish history. Outside and inside, this "grey romance in stone," as it has been called, speaks of the "old, unhappy, far-off times." It bears on its face the scars of repeated assaults and burnings; its fortunes have been bound up with those of the most brilliant and most unfortunate of the Stuarts—with the "Knight-errant King," who made its walls ring with mirth before he set out for Flodden; with the "Royal Martyr," who came here to be crowned; and with the "Young Chevalier," as well as with Mary and Darnley.

PRINCES STREET—LOOKING WEST

VIEW FROM NORTH BRITISH

STATION HOTEL

The southern wing of the Palace, and the screen which completes the quadrangle, are only modern in the sense that they belong to the later Jacobean period; they were begun in 1671, and conform in plan and features to the original design. The mysterious charm of Holyrood does not dwell in these State apartments; but there is some hope that they may again become an occasional residence of royalty, and that glimpses, at least, of the "brave days of old," may return to the Palace of the Stuarts, to the Abbey Quarter, and to the Old Town.

Not until a quarter of a century after Lochiel and his Highlanders slipped in through the Netherbow, and "Charlie sat in Geordie's chair" for a brief season, at Holyrood, did Edinburgh begin to build on its new stance across the valley. The foundation stone of the New Town was laid, not many yards from the base of the tower of the Station Hotel, in the year before Sir Walter Scott was born. From the beginning, this Northern Suburb, as it was then accounted, had the long terrace of Princes Street, its face turned to the south and to Old Edinburgh, as its base line; and at first it grew slowly. It was some time before traffic flowed freely over the gusty North Bridge, and, for a generation or two, the tide of commerce with Leith and the sea continued to "double the Cape," and flow through the deep and narrow channel of Leith Wynd, and the London stage coaches to roll out through the Water Gate towards Jock's Lodge and the Figgate Whins.

The site of the New Town is not unlike that of the Old, only in less bold relief, and turned the "other way round," with the Crags of Calton, in place of the Castle Rock, as its Acropolis. It is brandered in wide streets and "squares that court the breeze," across the gentle ridge along which once ran the country lane of the "Lang Gait," and on the slope down to the bed of the Water of Leith. Edinburgh has long ago stepped over that obstacle, and "flung her white arms" nearer and nearer to the sea. The city, indeed, has of late years effected a double lodgment on the shores of the Firth of Forth—to the east it has seized upon the seaside watering-place of Portobello, and to the north it has pushed down to Granton, hemming in closely on every side the port and burgh of Leith, which the capital long held in thrall.

In its growth, this stately Northern Edinburgh has surrounded and annexed many scenes of the rural life and industry of an earlier day, and their traces are not yet quite obliterated. Outside the New or Leith Wynd Port of the city lay, in those days, the little burgh of Calton; Waterloo Place, the eastward continuation of Princes Street, bestrides the site, and on the Dow Craig, alongside what is left of the Old Calton burying-ground that surrounded the Chapel of St Ninian, rise the battlemented turrets of the County Prison. The General Post Office occupies the place of "Shakespeare Square," where, even before the North Bridge was built and passable, the rank and fashion of Old Edinburgh flocked, by the steep way of Halkerston's Wynd, to the first licensed playhouse of the capital. The Register House rose on the site of the village of Moultrie Hill; further down the slope was Picardy, originally colonised by Huguenot silk-weavers, and the barony burgh of Broughton; while deep in the glen of the Water of Leith were the "Canonmills." named, like the neighbouring loch and village, after their owners, the Holyrood canons.

Leith Walk, at the time of the founding of the New Town, and for long after, was "the favourite path by which the citizen strolled when bent on an oyster feast and taking the air on Leith Pier"; it followed the line of the entrenchments raised by General Leslie against Cromwell's army, and led past Greenside and its eerie "Gallow Lee." From opposite the spot where stands the New Hotel, "Gabriel's Loan" meandered down the slope to the ford at Silvermills, after leaving behind Ambrose's Tavern, the scene of the meetings of Christopher North, the Ettrick Shepherd, and the rest of the joyous company of the "Noctes." Further west, indeed at the extreme end of Princes Street, the Kirk Loan led—by hawthorn hedges from the West Kirk, and from the kirkyard where Napier, the inventor of logarithms, and De Quincy, the "Opium-Eater," are among the sleepers—to the water-side at Stockbridge. Many trod it on their way to the mineral spring of St Bernard; others diverged by the road to the Queen's Ferry, which dived down to the group of ancient mills and quaint houses of the village of Dean, or wandered round by Bell's Mills. Those were days long before the gorge of the Water of Leith was spanned by the Dean Bridge, which now affords so magnificent a *coup d'œuil* to the traveller bound, by road, to the Forth Bridge.

The ground, now covered by the New Town, retained much of its rural aspect until well into last century. The city halted for a time on the line of Queen Street, which was the favourite Mall where Lord Cockburn, Lord Jeffrey, and their legal and literary associates strolled of an evening, admiring "the open prospect over the Forth and the north-western mountains." Fishing and wild-fowling were to be had in Canonmills Loch; at St Bernard's, Sir Henry Raeburn lived, well out into the country, and enjoyed a rural walk to his studio in York Place; and even after "feuing" had began on the further side of the Water of Leith, Thomas Carlyle could congratulate himself, as he smoked his pipe in the remote seclusion of Comely Bank, where he and his young wife had begun housekeeping, that he lived far from "the uproars and putrescences of the reeky town," whose lights only showed over the knowe against the dusky sky.

Many green and open spaces remain. One is the bosky Queen Street Gardens; another is the dell of the Water of Leith—sacred to the wanderings of David Balfour and Allan Breck Stewart—which keeps much of its natural beauty and something of its romance to this day. But Mrs Oliphant's complaint that "doleful lines of handsome houses weigh down the cheerful hillside under tons of monotonous stone," is not without cause. The New Town is handsome, stately, and well built;

but, beside Auld Reekie, it has undoubtedly an air of prim formality, of highly respectable and somewhat dull uniformity. It is, however, rapidly freeing itself from the reproach of a too-obtrusive symmetry of plan and line, with which its original builders endowed it.

The prevailing material, the white sandstone of Craigleith, tones softly, if slowly, into the ground-colour of the "grey metropolis"; the many fine features of its architecture are set out to the best advantage and in the best light. Noble structures have been reared, on superb sites, to religion, to art, and to education. From its "Close," in the most "West-endy" part of the city, rises the spire of St Mary's Episcopal Cathedral, beside the antique form of the Jacobean manor house of

Easter Coates, the lands of which have endowed this, the "first Scottish Cathedral built since the Reformation." The dome of St George's Parish Church—a miniature St Paul's—closes, to the west, the fine vista of George Street, with monuments occupying the centres of its squares and its crossings; and, neighbouring the lofty fluted column in St Andrew Square, surmounted by a colossal statue of Henry Dundas, Lord Melville, is the needle-like spire of St Andrew, from beneath which issued, in procession, the Fathers of the Disruption, to found the Free Church. Breaking the cold and severe grey range of the Queen Street houses, stands the National Portrait Gallery and Antiquarian Museum, a structure of warm red sandstone, in the fourteenth century Gothic style, bestowed

NORTH BRITISH STATION HOTEL AND
PRINCES STREET—LOOKING EAST

by the late Mr Findlay of Aberlour, as a storehouse of the treasures of Scottish portraiture and history. Further afield, in the directions north and west, in which Edinburgh has spread towards the wooded sides of Corstorphine Hill and towards the sea, rise the pinnacles and spires of Donaldson's Hospital, Fettes and Stewart's Colleges, and other fine buildings dedicated to Edinburgh's " chief industry"—the teaching of youth. Nor has the New Town reason to be ashamed of the imposing array of its banks and insurance offices, its shops and warehouses, its clubs, its hotels.

Already, as has been indicated, it has gathered its rich and deep store of literary associations; and, in the list of men of letters, art, and science, who have lived and worked in it, the New Town need hardly shrink from comparison with Old Edinburgh itself. "It is the later Edinburgh of Walter Scott and Lockhart, of the 'Blackwood Group' and the Edinburgh Reviewers. David Hume came to live at the corner of St Andrew Square—was not St David Street named after him in jest? Robert Burns lodged in St James Square, and penned epistles to 'Clarinda' in a high upper room looking down upon the green space behind the Register House. The bulk of the Waverley Novels were written at No. 39 North Castle Street, neighbours across the way marvelling at the daily vision of the hand that travelled ceaselessly across the paper. The 'Chaldee Manuscript' was concocted in John Wilson's house in Queen Street."

Of a later date were De Quincy, the genial Dr John Brown, Professor Blackie, and many a famous name besides, in the annals of art and literature, of medicine and philosophy, of law and divinity. But more, perhaps, even than Sir Walter himself, the author of "David Balfour" has made himself the "genius loci" of the New Town. Stevenson was born in Howard Place, off Inverleith Row; his father's house, while he was attending school and college, and giving fitful attention to law and engineering, was in Heriot Row. His spirit, even in exile, haunted the banks of the Water of Leith, the Queen Street Gardens, and the Calton Hill.

It is "R. L. S." who, with his conjuring rod, calls up for us the picture of Edinburgh, by day and by night, as seen from the Calton—that wonderful and enthralling picture, varying with every change in the weather or the light, and with every shifting of the point of view, which embraces the Old Town and the New, commands the vista of Princes Street, and looks down into the murkiest depths of the city closes, and out and away to the sea and the everlasting hills. From the vision of the Fife towns " each in its bank of blowing smoke," the Bass and the May and the seaway to the Baltic, "you turn to the city, and see the children dwarfed, by distance, to pigmies at play about suburban doorsteps; you have a glimpse upon a thoroughfare where people are densely moving; you note ridge after ridge of chimney-stalks running down-hill, one behind another, and church spires rising bravely from the sea of roofs. And here, you are on this pastoral hillside, among nibbling sheep and looked down upon by monumental buildings." Or if the visit be after nightfall, the lighted town shining up out of the darkness makes a spectacle as stimulating as that seen from "the hoariest summit of the Alps." "Moving lights on the railway pass and repass below the stationary lights on the bridge. Lights burn in the jail. Lights burn high up on the tall lands and on the Castle turrets; they burn low in Greenside and along the Park. They run out one beyond

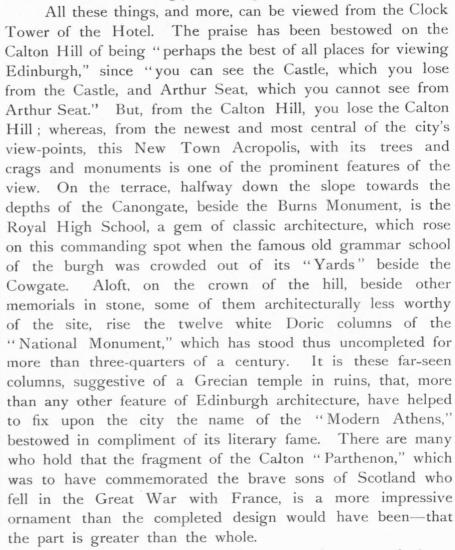

Scott Monument

another into the dark country. They walk in procession down to Leith, and shine singly far along Leith pier."

All these things, and more, can be viewed from the Clock Tower of the Hotel. The praise has been bestowed on the Calton Hill of being "perhaps the best of all places for viewing Edinburgh," since "you can see the Castle, which you lose from the Castle, and Arthur Seat, which you cannot see from Arthur Seat." But, from the Calton Hill, you lose the Calton Hill; whereas, from the newest and most central of the city's view-points, this New Town Acropolis, with its trees and crags and monuments is one of the prominent features of the view. On the terrace, halfway down the slope towards the depths of the Canongate, beside the Burns Monument, is the Royal High School, a gem of classic architecture, which rose on this commanding spot when the famous old grammar school of the burgh was crowded out of its "Yards" beside the Cowgate. Aloft, on the crown of the hill, beside other memorials in stone, some of them architecturally less worthy of the site, rise the twelve white Doric columns of the "National Monument," which has stood thus uncompleted for more than three-quarters of a century. It is these far-seen columns, suggestive of a Grecian temple in ruins, that, more than any other feature of Edinburgh architecture, have helped to fix upon the city the name of the "Modern Athens," bestowed in compliment of its literary fame. There are many who hold that the fragment of the Calton "Parthenon," which was to have commemorated the brave sons of Scotland who fell in the Great War with France, is a more impressive ornament than the completed design would have been—that the part is greater than the whole.

Here, on the Clock Tower, where we have chosen to take our outlook on Edinburgh, Old and New, we gaze full on the "fair face" of the City. Princes Street is before us in all its shining length. Away to the west, a group of spires and towers crowns the perspective, and balances the Calton columns—they are the spire of St Mary's Cathedral, the campanile of Free St George's, the Perpendicular tower of St John's Episcopal, and, at a lower level, almost under the giant shadow

Arthurs Seat & St Anthonys Chapel

of the Rock, the steeple of "St Cuthbert under the Castle." Besides the new Station Hotel, the only edifices that are permitted to stand thus front-to-front with Princes Street, are Walter Scott's Monument and the Royal Institution. This latter, a structure in "the Doric style of Pericles," where the School of Art is housed, and the Board of Manufactures has its headquarters, occupies the foot of the Mound, and, with the beautiful Ionic temple of the National Picture Gallery standing behind it, seems to join, by a graceful range of classic pillars and architraves, the New Town with the Old. But Edinburgh and Princes Street are still more proud of the Scott Monument—a pure and lovely embodiment of the spirit of Gothic art, and of the spirit of the great Master of Romance, designed by an almost self-taught artisan architect, George Meikle Kemp — over-canopying Steell's seated statue of Sir Walter, and enriched by sculptures from other hands.

There are many ways of viewing Princes Street, and many ideas of how and where it may be seen at its best. Alexander Smith preferred to take his stand at the corner of St Andrew Street, where one could watch "the puppets of the busy many-coloured hour move about on the pavement; while, across the ravine, time has piled the Old Town ridge on ridge, grey as a rocky coast, washed and worn by the foam of centuries." But the North British Station Hotel and its Clock Tower had not then risen to afford yet finer vantage for perusing "the poem of Princes Street." Most people may choose to scan it on a sunny day of summer or autumn, when, as R. L. Stevenson writes, the street is to be "seen in its glory," and Edinburgh, "with the soft air coming from the inland hills, military music sounding bravely from the hollow of the Gardens, and the flags all waving on its palaces," it is "what Paris ought to be."

But squall, and mist, and driving rain, somewhat too familiar visitants of Princes Street, do not rob it of its peculiar charms ; indeed, to some who have loved and studied its changeful face, its inconstancy of mood, the evanescence of its smiles has seemed to be most powerful of its spells. "After all," it has been written, "gay and garish sunshine is neither its most characteristic nor its most becoming dress. When the rosy morning light, stealing past the shoulder of Arthur Seat, strikes upon the Old Town projections and the buttresses of the Castle, and slowly gilds the sleeping front and deserted pavement of Princes Street, the effect is magical. The scene is not less lovely when flooded with mellow evening radiance. But, most entrancing of all, is the spectacle on a clear, starlight night, when the moon has just gone down behind the Castle battlements, and Old Edinburgh's ridged and chimneyed bulk of blackness is silhouetted against the midnight sky, like the ragged edge of a thunder-cloud."

NORTH BRITISH STATION HOTEL Edinburgh

ENTRANCE HALL FROM PRINCES STREET

THE
NORTH BRITISH STATION HOTEL.

HE North British Station Hotel, from its central and detached position, from its mass and height, and from its function as the complement and the crown of the Waverley Station, might be described as "the Hub" of Edinburgh. It stands, as has been said, at the geographical and commercial heart of the city. It is the chief architectural feature of Edinburgh's chief and most fashionable thoroughfare. It has its roots sunk almost at the lowest level of the deep hollow between the Old and New Towns; and its crest is reared above all but a few of the city spires. As a building, it is an ornament even to Edinburgh; as a hotel, it is one of the largest and best-appointed in the Kingdom.

The Hotel has the privilege of occupying the only stance reserved for a dwelling or place of business on the south side of Princes Street. It fills the eye to those who gaze along the vista from the west, and holds a still more dominating position when viewed from the east end of the great promenade and shopping mart of the New Town. The site is nearly square —180 feet by 190 feet—and the building rises ten storeys in height from the lowest basement floor to the roof—four storeys below, and six above, the level of Princes Street—to take no account of the Clock Tower, which crowns the edifice, and affords the unsurpassable series of prospects which have been

described in the previous section. As for its immediate surroundings, it fronts the north, and has its principal entrance in Princes Street, having opposite to it the Register House, the repository of the deeds and records of the Kingdom—a fine structure erected, from the designs of Adam, in 1774—and other buildings which, when they first rose, a century and a quarter ago, formed the nucleus of Princes Street and of New Edinburgh. To the east, the Hotel buildings line and—with the General Post Office facing them—form the entrance from the north to the North Bridge Street, out of which enter the Buffet and Grill Room of the Hotel.

The windows at the north-east angle of the building command at once the approaches to Leith and to the Calton Hill, by Leith Street and by Waterloo Place; from the corresponding angle on the south-east, springs the arch of the North Bridge, and the view extends over it, and over Holyrood and the Canongate, to Arthur Seat and Salisbury Crags. Southwards, the Hotel, founded on the Railway Station below, faces the new *Scotsman* premises, and the soaring and picturesque masses of the High Street houses; and, with these, and with the other buildings congregated on either side of North Bridge, it composes and makes a striking feature of one of the most impressive and handsome groups of street architecture to be found in Europe. On its west side it is skirted by the Waverley Steps—plunging down to the Station—to which it presents a range of shops; beyond this crowded stairway is the roof of the Waverley Market, a favourite lounge and resting-place, with seats and sward and pot-plants, on which the public rooms of the Hotel look directly down; and beyond this foreground the view embraces the whole of the noble front of Princes Street; the Scott Monument, the Mound, and the Gardens; the Lawnmarket and Castle Hill houses, and the Castle itself, crowning the Old Town; the group of West End spires and towers, and the hills behind.

BUFFET

The design of the Hotel is by the late Mr W. Hamilton Beattie, aided by Mr A. R. Scott, and completed under the care of Messrs Scott & Beattie, architects. It is "a free rendering of the Renaissance period," in which the architects have taken every advantage of the facilities which this style presents for linking, in a masterly

manner, "the old Scottish architecture of the Old Town with the rather severe classical architecture of the New." From its position of detachment, commanding and commanded by the chief avenues of Edinburgh's traffic and fashion, these features can be viewed to full advantage, and are never likely to be obscured.

To Princes Street, the edifice offers a front 190 feet in length, and rising, from street to roof, to a height of 100 feet, above which rears the great square Tower, whose "corona" is at an altitude of 195 feet above the pavement, and 248 feet above the base on the railway level. The six storeys above the street level are built around a quadrangular central court, about 70 feet square, in which, on the ground floor, is placed a dome-roofed Palm Lounge; and the four great elevations which the Hotel presents to the four points of the compass are treated with much freedom, but in harmonious subordination to the general design.

"Horizontally, the dominant lines of the building are suitably emphasised by means of balustrades and carved bands, while, on a level with the fourth floor from the street, is the main cornice, with massive dentils and an embattled parapet, broken up at intervals by turrets. Another salient feature is formed by the angle pavilions, which, ending in cupolas, surrounded by turrets, at the roof level, flank the tower at each corner of the building, and give variety and unity to the design. The general treatment of the main elevation is fairly bold in the lower storeys.

GRILL ROOM

Arched windows, effectively grouped in fours, appear on the first and second floors, on each side of the central tower; on the two higher storeys, the windows are square-headed, and above that, the treatment is of a lighter and more ornate description. Above the main cornice and parapet, the two storeys are treated with dormer windows, possessing several elegant features, so that the line at the wall head is picturesque and interesting." The Clock Tower itself has a comparatively plain shaft, terminating in an arched cornice with corbelling at the angles, over which rise corner turrets finished by coroneted cupolas, and enclosing a clock face, surmounted by a pediment, on each of the four sides. Above these is a steep lead-covered timber roofing, with a balustrade on top, reached from the interior by a spiral iron stair, and completed by a leaden corona and a

flagstaff. It is finely proportioned, and conveys suggestions of the campanile tower, of the Scottish baronial castle, and finally, of the mural crown of St Giles.

On the other three sides, "the angle pavilions with their finely designed oriels and turreted cupolas are the same as on the front elevations. To balance these, a feature has been made of the gable which projects in the centre of each elevation, to correspond with the central tower of the main front, and it is finished at the top with a tympanum and niche. On the east elevation, that to North Bridge Street, where there is a line of shops on the street level and a mezzanine floor above, the treatment of the details is of a flatter description." The four basement storeys, below the Princes Street level, are naturally of a much plainer character externally.

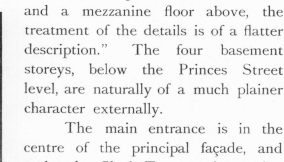

Entrance Hall

The main entrance is in the centre of the principal façade, and under the Clock Tower. A massive portico, flanked by twin columns, surmounts the doorway, and leads into the magnificent Main Entrance Hall. But it may be more convenient to make the first acquaintance with the interior of the building, by means of the approach specially provided for the guests who arrive by rail in the station below. By lift or a stair entered from the north corner of the west front of the Booking Hall, a Covered Way or Corridor, on the level of the second basement floor of the Hotel, is reached. The Corridor is lighted from above, and is artistically decorated with shrubs and plants; its sides are trellised, and vines and clematis are already twining on this wood-work. It leads to the Arrival Hall, a large and handsome room, of noteworthy aspect and design, divided into six compartments by reeded alabaster columns supported by pedestals or set on dados of Numidian marble, with bréche-clair bases and cornices, which run around the walls, while the floor is of slabs of Sicilian marble alternating with bréche-clair.

Here the visitor can book his rooms, and be conveyed by electric passenger

PALM COURT OR LOUNGE

elevator to whatever floor of the Hotel he pleases. But, for purposes of description, it will be better to make our approach to these upper storeys by returning to the Main Entrance and Entrance Hall.

This is a spacious apartment, entered by a "Van Kannel," or turnstile door. It is 50 feet long, by 22 feet wide, and 20 feet high. The floor consists of panels of Sicilian and blue-belge marble; the ceiling is richly panelled in plaster; the walls are divided into compartments by fluted pilasters, with decorated panels intervening. Advantage has been taken of the mezzanine floor to form a gallery, with open balustrade, in this Hall.

A short flight of steps here leads to the Palm Court or Lounge. It is a fine hall, 50 feet square, flanked by eliptical bays on the four sides, and lighted from the roof by an octagonal dome filled in with leaded and coloured glass and panelled in plaster. The dome is supported at the four corners of the Lounge by fluted columns, cabled at the foot, and having highly enriched capitals. Pilasters of the same type divide the room into fourteen separate bays, with panelling

Staircase & Elevator

and mirrors between; and the two central panels are filled with impressive oil paintings by the eminent French artist, M. Olivier Merson, emblematical of "Peace" and "War." Over the door, at either end, is a balcony, entered from the mezzanine floor above, and affording a charming view of the room, which is provided with many lounges, chairs and tables, and ornamented with palms.

Branching from the Main Entrance Hall to the right, or west, and forming, as it were, a wing of it, is the Grand Staircase Hall. It resembles, in style and decoration, the apartment from which it diverges, although it is somewhat lower in the roof. On its south side is the spacious Main Staircase, communicating both with the floors above and with the basement floors below, and the electric elevators which provide a still easier and more rapid means of access to all parts of the building.

In these outer courts of the Hotel, as they may be called, one expects to find the key to the internal plan and arrangements of the building. The "vital requirements of a good hotel plan" are laid down by the original architect in his description of his design. The conditions required include "straight, well-lighted corridors, and easy and readily-found staircases and elevators"; that "the guest on arrival must be able at once to reach the office, to procure

SMOKING ROOM

his room, and to proceed there direct without detour or delay"; that "the hotel offices should command the principal entrances"; that "the public rooms should command the best views, and should be in such positions as are most convenient for the special class of guests who chiefly use them"; that "the smoking and billiard rooms should be in readily accessible, but retired situations, where they do not interfere with the comfort of the lady guests"; that "the kitchen should be large, well lighted and ventilated, and in a central position," with the administrative apartments clustered round it in a compact and easily accessible plan; that the bedrooms should be of good size, and varied in dimensions, and on all the principal floors there should be "suites of

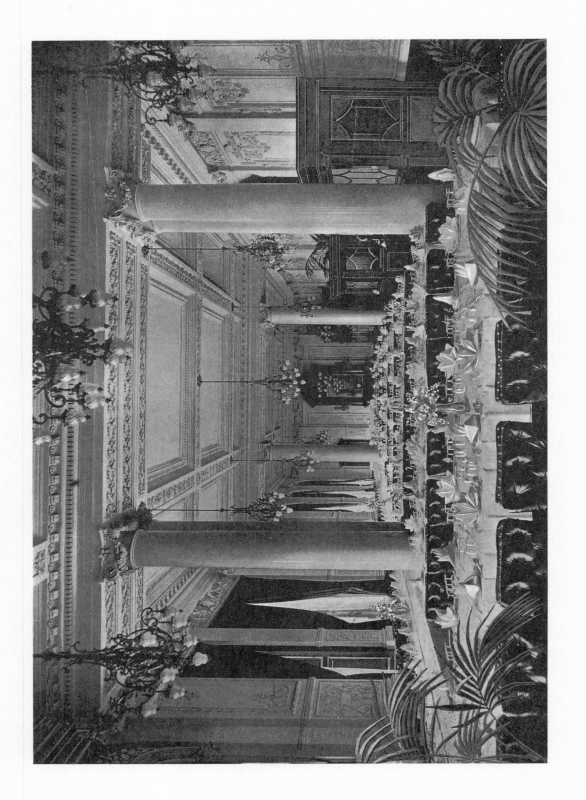

sitting-rooms, bedrooms, dressing-rooms and bathrooms to meet the needs of travellers"; that "careful provision should be made for the rapid and efficient service of both the private sitting rooms and bedrooms upon each floor, and for prompt attendance on visitors' rooms, both by day and night"; that "everything connected with the hotel should, as far as possible, be done upon the premises"; that provision should be made for a restaurant business; that stocks of wines and spirits should be kept and matured on the premises; and that careful arrangements should be made for the housing and comfort of the hotel servants. All these and other requirements of the ideal hotel have not only been aimed at, but have been realised, and worked-out in elaborate detail, in the new building.

We may now enter the chief public room of the Hotel—the principal Dining Room—which opens off the Grand Staircase Hall on the street floor, and occupies the centre of the west front, overlooking the garden-roof of the Waverley Market. It is an apartment of noble proportions and pleasing aspect, measuring 112 feet in length by 35 feet in width, and 20 feet in height, the ceiling being carried on four twin-columns. The walls are partly panelled in mahogany and partly in decorated plaster-work; the supporting pillars are white; the ceiling design is on simple and dignified lines; and over the entrance porch of this great dining hall is placed a gallery for an orchestra. The Kitchen, with servery, scullery, and still-room, immediately adjoins the Dining Room to the east, and has access to it by two entrances, enclosed by mahogany screens with swing doors. The cooking apparatus and appliances are of the most modern and complete description. The close proximity of the Kitchen to the Dining Room gives unusual facilities for prompt service; while the heat and fumes of the "cuisine" are effectually excluded.

Immediately to the south of the principal Dining Room is one of smaller dimensions and similar decoration, for private dinners; it is designed to be used also as a Ball Room. In the centre of the south front, on the same floor, is a spacious Writing and Reading Room, 42 feet long, by 21 feet wide, lined, to a height of $7\frac{1}{2}$ feet, with a panelled mahogany dado, and lighted by two large oriel and two smaller windows. The ceiling has a fine oval centre panel, with enriched plaster beams, and with cornice and frieze; and the commodious and comfortable room has, among its other attractions, that of being quiet and retired, and of commanding a prospect of exceptional interest and beauty.

The Drawing Room lies to the west of the Main Entrance, looks out upon Princes Street, and enters from the Grand Staircase Hall. It is a beautifully decorated and upholstered apartment of handsome proportions, measuring 71 feet 6 inches in length, by 27 feet in width. Its ceiling, like those of the principal Dining Room and Ball Room, is divided into square

THE NORTH BRITISH STATION HOTEL—
LOOKING WEST

compartments with massive plaster beams, enriched by ornament. Its walls are divided by pilasters which respond to the ceiling beams, and the panels between the pilasters are embellished by festoons of fruits and flowers, and surrounded by ornamental mouldings. The lower part of the walls is finished with mahogany panelled dados, while the chimney-pieces have overmantels with mirrors, fluted Corinthian pilasters, and handsome pediments.

In the first basement floor below is a Smoking Lounge of spacious dimensions; and this portion of the Hotel may be regarded as devoted to the solace and recreation, and to the business wants, of the male section of the visitors. Here are the two admirably appointed Billiard Rooms; the "American Bar"; the Commercial Travellers' Writing Room and Stock Rooms, and extensive lavatory accommodation.

The plan of each of the floors above the street level is practically the same, and is easily grasped. The building being almost square, the corridors run at right angles to each other around the whole structure, and terminate at three of the corners with an octagonal hall or lobby, well lighted from the roof by a large glass cupola; while the fourth corner—the north-west—is occupied by the Grand Staircase, a

BILLIARD ROOM

spacious flight of granolithic steps, extending from the first basement storey to the roof. The staircase has a handsome wrought-iron and brass balustrade and massive mahogany handrail, and is lighted by a cupola on the roof, and by windows enriched with stained glass of heraldic design, bearing the Scottish Lion and the Castle of the capital city. It is also illuminated, in the lower storeys, by an ingenious device of "artificial sunlight," produced by electric lamps reflected from behind thick glass.

Off the corridors, on either hand, open doors that give admission to bedrooms and other apartments, lighted either from the outer side or from the inner court. The First Floor, on the west side, is wholly devoted to

SUITE OF
PRIVATE SITTING
ROOM,
BEDROOM AND
BATHROOM

a suite of six public rooms, which can be used separately, or thrown open from end to end, and consisting of Music Room—at the Princes Street extremity—and Drawing and Dining Rooms. All of them command fine prospects of Princes Street and its Gardens; all of them are decorated, with notable grace and effect, in white, with richly panelled ceilings, doors, mantelpieces, and mirrored overmantels, in the "Adam" style, and of diverse designs. On the same floor, over the Main Entrance, and on the south and east sides, are four large private drawing rooms or sitting rooms, decorated in ornate French and Italian styles, capable of being used "en suite" in conjunction with the adjoining

PRIVATE DRAWING ROOM

bedrooms and bathrooms. A feature of the arrangements on this floor, and on the floors above, is the facility with which the rooms can be used either separately or in suite of bedrooms and bathroom, or of bedrooms, bathroom and sitting room; while the apartments opening upon the octagonal corner halls can be so connected and isolated as to give all the home-like privacy of a self-contained flat.

On all the floors special and ample bath and lavatory accommodation has been provided; there are Ladies' and Gentlemen's Hairdressing Rooms, in the north-east corner of the First Floor, and two or three house-maids' rooms on each flat. On the sixth storey from the street the female staff of the Hotel are comfortably housed ; and in the Tower, under the Clock, are the tanks that hold the principal part of the water supply of the premises, pumped up thither by engines in the third basement.

A few facts, figures, and dimensions may be given to indicate the magnitude and the character of the whole undertaking. The total number of rooms, including cellars, in the Hotel is 700 ; of these over 300 are bedrooms. About 13,000 tons of stone, 1,600 tons of steel girders, and 8 millions of bricks have been employed in the building. There are 26 acres of plaster work ; the floors cover an area of 6½ acres ; there are 24 miles of cornices and 15 miles of skirtings. The number of windows in the structure runs up to 1000, and of doors to 2000. The electric tubing extends to 50 miles, and the number of electric lamps is about 5000, possessing in the aggregate 24,000 candle-power. The total length of hot, cold, main supply, fire main, soil, waste, and ventilation pipes is about 25 miles. Two hot-water heaters supply 2000 gallons of hot water each per hour ; the domestic and reserve water supply is about 75,000 gallons, and there are in all 52 baths and 70 lavatories. The wine cellars, situated on the second basement floor, are very spacious and complete, and contain vats holding matured whiskies, and a very large stock of carefully-selected wines. Ventilation and heating are on the " Plenum " System, and the ventilating fans draw in from 14 to 18 millions of cubic feet of air per hour, by which means the atmosphere throughout the building is every hour renewed from four to six times. This atmosphere, on the coldest day, will be maintained at a uniform temperature of 60 degrees Fahrenheit. Each clock-face in the Tower is over 13 feet in diameter ; the minute-hand is 6 feet 3 inches, and the hour-hand 4 feet 6 inches, in length ; the clock is lighted by electricity by means of an ingenious self-acting apparatus.

The Hotel is absolutely fireproof throughout, and as little inflammable material has been used in its construction as possible ; so that if a fire should arise at any point, it would have difficulty in spreading, while the spacious corridors and staircases would give easy facilities for leaving the building in safety. As a further preventative, the building is fitted throughout with fire stations, and has hydrants and hose in each corridor. In each bedroom a framed and glazed plan of its respective flat is hung up, with the room indicated in red colour, and with printed instructions of what should be done in case of fire breaking out. There are four fire stations on every floor, one in the centre of each corridor, each supplied with hydrant, hose, pails, portable fire pumps, firemen's tools, &c., complete. On the fire alarm being rung, it summons the firemen, who are on duty day and night. The water supply for the fire mains is stored in a tank at the bottom of the Tower, and they are also connected with the tanks on the sixth floor level. There are in all 41 fire stations on the premises.

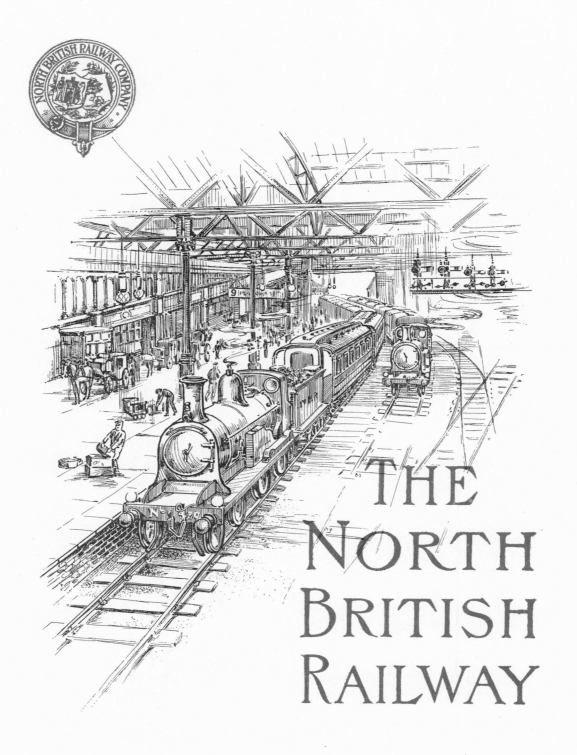

THE
NORTH
BRITISH
RAILWAY

MELROSE ABBEY

THE NORTH BRITISH RAILWAY.

HE Hotel impends over the Waverley Station—the centre and tap-root of the North British Railway. Its guests are placed at the very source and fountainhead of a system that, through its main trunk and many branches and connections of rail, coach and steamer, can transport them, at will, to any corner of broad Scotland, or "o'er the Border and awa'." Is it the wish to visit classic Hawthornden or romantic Abbotsford; to wander by ballad-haunted Yarrow and Ettrick, or on the banks of Loch Lomond; to be landed at the root of Ben Ledi or Lochnagar; to tread the coasts of Fife or the shores of Skye; to set eyes on Neidpath or Branxholm, St Andrews or Stirling, the Carse of Gowrie or the Moor of Rannoch, Rob Roy's Cave or the Brigs o' Ayr, Thrums or Drumtochtie?—the magic word has but to be spoken at the Waverley Station.

From the Waverley, the rails ray out to all points of the compass, like the threads of a spider's web, and invade and traverse alike the busiest and the most picturesque and solitary parts of Scotland. The East Coast route and the Waverley route offer alternative roads into England, each, in its own way, of transcendent interest; the Forth Bridge and the Tay Bridge are steel links in a wonderful chain of communication that stretches across sea and land towards Dundee and Aberdeen; by Stirling and Dunblane, rapid and easy access is had to the Trossachs and Scotland's most celebrated "Lake District"; through Glenfarg and Perth goes the direct way across the Grampians to the capital of the Highlands, and beyond it to the neighbourhood of John o' Groats;

DOWN MAIN PLATFORM

Glasgow and the busy industrial towns and watering-places of the Clyde may be reached by way either of Falkirk or of Bathgate; and by the shores of the Gareloch and Loch Lomond, and on by the Black Mount and the base of Ben Nevis to "Prince Charlie's country" in Glenfinnan and Morar, runs the new West Highland Railway, through mountain scenery of unsurpassable loveliness, till it reaches the coast opposite to Skye.

These main streams of tourist travel we shall glance along by and by. But the Waverley Station is fed also by a host of minor tributaries, branch lines, long and short, some of which open up scenes of beauty and note in the immediate neighbourhood of Edinburgh, and may be easily visited by residents at the Station Hotel "between meals." Then the Suburban line sweeps round the whole southern outskirts of the city, bringing the traveller into touch with the Water of Leith and Craiglockhart, with the Braid and Blackford Hills, and with Duddingston and Craigmillar Castle; and it forms one of the many means of access from the Waverley to the pier and sands and golf links of Portobello, Edinburgh's newly annexed suburb and sea-bathing resort, which is wont to call itself "the Brighton of the North." A neighbour of another type is reached in a few minutes by the line to Leith, once the vassal port and the hereditary enemy of the Capital, now a large and stirring place of commerce, with magnificent docks filled with shipping and merchandise from the Continent and all parts of the world, yet still possessing in the vicinity of the Kirkgate, the Sandgate and the Shore, many relics of its past. From the "Pier of Leith" there are excursions by steamer to the ancient sanctuary of the May, around the rock-prison of the Bass, the modern fortress of Inchkeith, and the ruined priory of Inchcolm, under the giant limbs of the Forth Bridge, and to many other spots of old romance and of scenic beauty scattered over the shores and islands of the "gallant Firth." By Granton also, the Railway Company's steamer service on the Burntisland ferry, transports those who would to Fife by water.

There are other short lines that conduct those who are on pleasure or business bent, to Corstorphine, a pleasant village with a venerable church, nestling under its hill, or to Musselburgh, an "honest toun" at the mouth of the Esk, that boasts of its antiquity, of its literary memories, and of a golf links of renown. Nor does anybody visit Edinburgh, and has time to spare, who does not find his way to Roslin, with its ruined Castle, once the seat of "the lordly line of high St Clair," nodding over a reach of the North Esk, and behind it the Chapel, most exquisitely chased of the gems of the Gothic art of its period. Not far off, and overlooking the romantic dell of the same historic stream, is Hawthornden, where Wallace found hiding in the cave, and where Drummond and rare Ben Jonson walked and talked of things said and done "at the Mermaid."

Roslin and its environs may be reached by no fewer than four railway routes—by the direct line that ends at Glencorse, under the shadow of the

UP MAIN PLATFORM (EAST END), WAVERLEY STATION

BOOKING HALL

Pentland Hills; by the branch to Polton at the foot of the Dell; and by the Penicuik or the Peebles line, the former of which brings one into the close vicinity of the scenes in the "Gentle Shepherd," while the other sends out an offshoot that passes behind the green screen of the Pentlands to West Linton, seated where the Lyne Water rushes down from the "Cauldstaneslap."

Nearer at hand, where these branches join the main line, and where the two Esks meet, is Dalkeith, planted at the Duke of Buccleuch's Palace gates, and having Newbattle Abbey, Lord Lothian's fine seat, as an equally close neighbour. In another direction, to the westward, other two lordly mansions, with spacious grounds accessible to the visitor, are within easy reach of Dalmeny, where above the picturesquely huddled houses of South Queensferry, the Forth Bridge "takes off" for its spring to the opposite bank. They are Dalmeny House, the Scottish home of the Earl of Rosebery, and Hopetoun House, the stately seat of the Marquis of Linlithgow; each is placed amidst noble trees, lawns and deer parks, in proximity to the Forth; each has its older castle, restored or in ruin, still closer to the sea marge, and each has near it a venerable Norman church.

LINLITHGOW PALACE AND LOCH

Linlithgow Palace, too, the birthplace of unfortunate Mary Stuart, the favourite resort of old-time Scottish monarchy, stands above the loch and beside the ancient Church of St Michael's, within "thirty minutes of the Waverley"; so do a score of other places of old renown, whose charm has been increased, not impaired, by years. Are their names and their chronicles not written in the guide books?

THE EAST COAST ROUTE.

WHEN one proceeds to survey the main lines of travel that converge on the Waverley Station, it is natural that preference should be given to the original track of the North British Railway, that is the East Coast Route; the direct road into England, which, according to Dr Samuel Johnson, the Scotsman always takes most readily. The Great North Road keeps, roughly speaking, alongside the railway track, sometimes crossing it, often wandering away from it, but never wandering very far. In days long before the stage-coach, this way through the fertile country, lying between the hills and the sea, was the line taken by invading armies, English and Scottish; on it, the fate of kingdoms and dynasties has been decided, and battlefields are strewn along its course. The rails pass over or skirt the ground on which Pinkie Cleuch, Prestonpans, Dunbar, Halidon Hill and other famous fights were fought. Ancient castles, most of them now in ruin, stand close to the line; Fawside, Preston, Dolphinton, Redbraes, Fenton, Dunbar, and even the great baronial holds of Dirleton and Tantallon, are among those that can be glimpsed from the carriage windows by those who know when and where to look, in passing through East Lothian alone.

This region, between the pastoral Lammermoors and the sea, is the home of high farming and of golf. Noble mansions, Gosford, Tyninghame, and Beil among them, lie near the track, and the Prime Minister's seat of Whittinghame, with the old tower in which the Darnley tragedy was plotted, is close at hand, screened by Traprain Law, one of the many blocks of basalt, that start abruptly out of the fertile plain. The Garleton Hills hide the little county town of Haddington, reached by a branch line, where Knox was born and Jane Welsh Carlyle is buried under the ruined choir of the "Lamp of Lothian." The dark pyramid of North Berwick Law stands sentinel over the fashionable bathing resort behind it; and out of the sea itself signs of old volcanic forces crop up in the shape of the Bass and other islands.

Here, too, is what has been called the "Holy Land of Golf." Breezy expanses of turf and bent and sand fringe the coast from Aberlady eastward, and an ever-growing crowd of eager golfers throng, by the branch lines from Longniddry and Drem, to the links of Kilspindie, Luffness, Gullane, Muirfield, Archerfield and North Berwick. Golf resumes its reign for a brief space again at the ancient burgh of Dunbar, but afterwards the ground becomes too steep and rocky for the game; and the line itself draws away again from the shore, and threads its way through Cockburnspath pass and the beautiful wooded glen of the Pease burn, behind the high ground, terminating in the cliffs of St Abb's Head, that hide the "Wolf's Crag" of the "Bride of Lammermoor," and Coldingham Priory, until, having passed Ayton, it emerges, between the fishing villages of Eyemouth and Burnmouth, above the sounding coves and surf-beaten stacks of the Berwickshire coast.

BERWICK-UPON-TWEED

In little more than an hour's run, the long stage to Berwick, which used to occupy a day, is accomplished. Scotland is left behind at Lamberton toll—the Gretna Green of the Eastern Marches. But one feels, in a sense, in Northern territory while in "Berwick bounds" and on the north side of the Tweed. In the early days of the "North British," when it had planted its foot in Berwick-upon-Tweed, but before the section of line had been built which joined up the system with that of the North-Eastern and the Great Northern, the journey had still to be continued by coach; and the fare for the double trip between the Border and Newcastle was not less than that which the excursionist now pays for travelling from the Waverley to King's Cross and back. The opening, in 1850, of the great viaduct across the Border river, completing direct railway communication between Edinburgh and London, was "the last Act of Union." The walls and ramparts of Berwick preserve some memory of the "battles, sieges, fortunes," through which it has passed; of the bloody massacres and eventful conferences it has witnessed in the times when there was feud between the realms. In these peaceful days, it does a modest shipping, fishing and manufacturing business, and is not uninterested or unprofited by the tide of traffic, no longer tolled, that flows through it between Scotland and England.

THE WAVERLEY ROUTE.

THE other great track of the tourist, to or from the South, is that Midland or Waverley Route, which leads through the Border Country of Walter Scott to "Merry Carlisle." It strikes inland at Portobello, and beyond Dalkeith holds up the valley of the South Esk to the watershed on the Moorfoots, giving glimpses of Cockpen Kirk, and, to right and to left, of the tall grey Keep of Borthwick and of the ruined walls of Crichton Castle, commanding the Vale of Tyne, both of them associated with the fate and adventures of Mary Queen of Scots, and of her evil genius, Bothwell. Then under high green hills of pasture and rich corn lands, we speed down Gala Water,

ABBOTSFORD

crossing many times from bank to bank of that bickering stream, and through Bowland tunnel, emerge at Galashiels on Tweed side, in the very heart of the " Scott Country."

Across the Tweed is Abbotsford itself, the "enchanted castle" raised by the wand of the Wizard before his gains had turned to "fairy gold." No house is so charged with literary memories, so thronged with relics of "old romance." The spell still holds on it and on the country around. The spirit of Sir Walter, rightful heir and successor to True Thomas, the Rhymer, seems to sit enthroned on the triple Eildons. They look down upon Melrose and its Abbey—on "Kennaquhair" and "The Monastery"—scene of many Border frays between Scots and Southrons, and between Scotts and Kers, the home and fane of the Cistercian monks, burial place of the doughty Douglases and of Wise Michael and his magic book, more exquisitely beautiful and more pilgrim-haunted in its decay than in the days of its glory. Not far remote is Dryburgh, where, in a sweet seclusion of ivied ruin and cloistered shade, the weary Magician was laid to rest under sculptured stone and ruined arch. All around are spots whose very names—Ashiestiel, Torwoodlee, Yair, Darnick, Chiefswood, Glendearg, Bowden, Mertoun, Bemerside—are "words of power" that awaken memories of the forays and the ballads of the days of old, and of the story— saddest and most inspiring of any—of the Last Minstrel of this land of song and legend.

From Galashiels there is a branch line that, by Clovenfords, passes up the valley of the Tweed to Innerleithen (St Ronan's Well) and to Peebles, bringing within reach, on the main stream and its tributaries, Caddon, Leithen, Quair, Eddleston, Manor, Lyne and the rest, scenes innumerable, that are celebrated in Border history or have their place in ballad lore or in Waverley romance ; among the rest, Traquair and Neidpath and Drummelzier Castles, and the graves of Merlin and of the Black Dwarf. A short line follows the Ettrick to Selkirk, the old " Forest " capital, whose souters played their part so well at Flodden ; and thence, or from Innerleithen, approach can be made to the " Dowie Dens of Yarrow," and so on by St Mary's Loch and the Grey Mare's Tail to Moffat. From Selkirk the way winds " the green hills under," by Philiphaugh battlefield, by the Newark Castle of the " Lay," by Mungo Park's birth-place at Foulshiels, by Yarrow and St Mary's Kirks, by the Ettrick Shepherd's farms of Mountbenger and Altrive, by Dryhope and Henderland Towers, by Douglas and Meggat waters, the scenes of the " Douglas Tragedy " and the " Border Widow's Lament," and by the howff of Christopher North and his cronies at " Tibbie Shiels." Names, these, surely too eloquent with the note of woe or of mirth to need expansion. Or another road, scarcely less full charged with romance, can be taken, up Ettrick by Carterhaugh, Bowhill, Michael Scott's Tower, Tushielaw, Buccleuch Burn, and Thirlestane to Ettrick Kirk.

St Boswell's, at the foot of the Eildon Hills, is another junction from which diverging lines open up sections of the Border Country. The Berwick-shire Railway passes over the Tweed by the fine viaduct at Leaderfoot, to trace the lovely "Leader haughs" by Drygrange and Cowdenknowes as far as Earlston, the Ercildoune of Thomas the Rhymer, whose ivy-clad tower stands close to the line. From Lauderdale it passes on to join the East Coast route at Reston *via* Greenlaw and Duns, where a Scottish Covenanting army twice checkmated Charles I. The upper reaches of Leader and the little old-world burgh of Lauder have now a direct approach by a light railway from Fountainhall on Gala Water.

More important is the branch which keeps the right bank of the Tweed all the way to its mouth at Berwick. On the road it throws off a little side-line to Jedburgh, a pretty Border town which long held an ambiguous reputation for its justice and its staves. Its Abbey, partly restored by the Marquis of Lothian, whose house of Mounteviot is close by, rivals Melrose and Dryburgh in architectural beauty and interest. At Kelso, where Tweed and Teviot join, is the fourth of the great Border abbeys, a ponderous Norman fragment, half castle, half religious house, holding guard over the town and bridge of Kelso, the centre-piece of a noble landscape. Old Roxburgh Castle near by, was, in its day, a still stronger guard against incursion, or sharper thorn in the side of the Kingdom ; and it was opposite it, in the grounds of Floors Castle, the magnificent seat of the Duke of Roxburghe, that King James of the Fiery Face was slain by the bursting of a cannon.

The Peel of Smailholm, or Sandyknowe, the "shattered tower" that kindled the youthful fancy of Scott, seems to the traveller by this line to stalk like a sentinel on the heights beyond the river. Its place is afterwards taken by the massive form of Hume Castle, the old home of the Homes and key of the Merse, whose equivalent on the English side is Wark ; and half-way between these grim Border strengths, both now in ruin, is a monument that reminds us that Thomson, the gentle author of "The Seasons," was born at Ednam. To the South rises the Great Cheviot, crowning a range that is cloven by passes, once well-known to the Border thieves, leading up from the valleys of the Kale and Bowmount ; the Gipsy town of Kirk Yetholm hangs upon the English march ; and across the frontier, on the last buttress of the Cheviots, above the sullen Till, is Flodden Ridge, the field on which James IV. and his host were smitten on the "dowiest day" that ever befel Scotland. From Coldstream Bridge and Cornhill, in this neighbourhood, a line through Wooler opens up the hill country of Northumberland, and before the Berwick branch reaches Tweedmouth and the sea, it passes "the battled towers, the donjon keep" of Norham, and affords glimpses up the Whitadder, surpassed by no minor Border stream in wealth of charm and legend.

From St Boswells, on the Tweed, the main line crosses to Hawick, at the junction of the Slitrig and the Teviot, the halfway house to Carlisle. On the way, one sights the high ground on which the battle of Lilliard's Edge was fought, crosses Ale Water, and passes the Minto Crags. And so we come to the bounds of Teviotdale, a "perennial battlefield," like all the country round about, in the days of rugging and reiving, when the Bauld Buccleuch was Warden of the Marches at Branxholm; when Jamie Telfer of the Fair Dodhead "lowsed his kye" at Goldielands Tower, and Johnie Armstrong of Gilknockie, with all his following, were hung at Carlinrig. These spots are all on the Upper Teviot, on the road that goes by Mosspaul to Ewes Water and Langholm. But at hand also are Harden, where Auld Wat lived with the Flower of Yarrow and became ancestor of Walter Scott; Ormiston, whence rode to Border fray the Gledstanes, forebears of the famous Prime Minister; and Cavers, Stobs, and Minto, where Douglases and Elliots held more than feudal sway. Behind "dark Ruberslaw, rugged and hoary with the spoils of time," lies Rule Water, where there is a still wilder country lying close to the ridge of Cheviot and the English border, across which, at the Carter Bar, passes an old stage road to Reedsdale and Newcastle.

The rough vigour and enterprise of the Borderers have been turned into new channels — into pastoral farming; into art, science and literature; into the hosiery, tweed and other manufactures that have been planted at Galashiels, Selkirk and Hawick. But the old Hawick spirit is revived in pristine energy when the citizens unfurl their Flodden Banner and raise their war chant of "Teeriebus" at the Moat Hill on the day of the Common Riding.

Another watershed is passed, and the line is among streams winding down between green or heathery hills to the waters of the Solway. This is the valley of the Liddell, the very sanctuary of the Border freebooters. Lauriston, Riccarton, Mangerton, Whithaugh, are names redolent of the daring and lawless deeds of the Elliots and Armstrongs, now almost weeded out of the valley; and "thieves, robbers and Liddesdale men" were placed under the same ban in the old Scottish Acts. But no Border hold has so many dark traditions clinging about it as Hermitage Castle, on the Hermitage Water above Newcastletown, where Christie's Will hid a Lord of Session, where Mary, in an evil hour, rode to visit Bothwell, where the Knight of Liddesdale immured his prisoners, and where Lord Soulis was "lapped in lead" before being boiled on the Nine Stane Rig.

From Riccarton Junction a line crosses the Kieldar Heights and descends into the North Tyne, passing through a fine Border district to the Roman Wall, to Hexham and to Newcastle, and throwing off, at Reedsmouth, a cross-country

STIRLING CASTLE

branch which, at Scotsgap, meets the lines from Rothbury and Morpeth. The main route holds on down stream into and through the Debateable Land; enters England at Kershope Foot, sends out a branch from Riddings to Langholm; at Longtown stretches out a link across Solway Moss to Gretna Green, that opens communication with Annandale, Nithsdale and Galloway; crosses Esk and Eden, and lands the passenger under "Carlisle Castle wa'," at the gate of the English Lakes, on the fairway for Ireland by Silloth, and on the high road for St Pancras.

To the Scottish "Lake Country."

THE Highland Border is as easy of access from the Waverley Station as the Scottish Marches. Within an hour from Edinburgh the traveller can be at Stirling, on the threshold of the Land of the Gael and on the way to the Trossachs *via* the Clachan of Aberfoyle. He can either choose his route by the Forth Bridge, Dunfermline, and Alloa; or he may proceed through Polmont and Larbert. In the former case, he will come within reach of Culross, birthplace of St Mungo, and best preserved of ancient Fife burghs; will cross the Devon—or if it pleases him, explore its beautiful valley by Dollar, the "Castle of Gloom," and Rumbling Bridge, as far as Loch Leven—and pass between the foothills of the green Ochils and the Forth to the base of Stirling Rock. Or, should he take the direction followed of old by kings and armies—athwart West Lothian and the rich Carselands on the Southern side of Forth—he will cross, on his way, the valleys of the Almond, Avon, and Carron; he will brush close past Queen Mary's Niddrie and Linlithgow; he will obtain a glimpse from afar of the shipping ports of Bo'ness and Grangemouth, connected by branches with the main line; from Camelon he can give his attention, according to his tastes, to the remains of the Roman Wall or to the Carron Works; at Falkirk, Sauchie, and Bannockburn, he is close to the sites of famous battlefields.

The nearer one draws to "the towers of Snowdon" and Stirling Brig, the more majestic grows the scene and the more crowded the historic page. The monument on the Abbey Craig—"a feudal tower surmounted by a mural crown" —is a memorial of

> "Patriot battles won of old,
> By Wallace wight, and Bruce the bold,"

WALLACE MONUMENT

but more particularly of the exploits of the "Protector of Scotland," who was the victor at Stirling and the vanquished at Falkirk. Cambuskenneth Abbey, across the river from Stirling Station, and the Castle, looking down upon it from the crest of its fortified rock are, however, landmarks more worthy of note. "Forth bridled the wild Highlandman"; and Stirling Castle was the key that locked the gateway to intruders from either North or South. It was a watch-tower of the nearer Highlands, whose peaks, as seen from "Queen Mary's Lookout," are grouped around it in a great half-circle; while "the mazy Forth" can be seen unravelled at its feet. The story of Castle, Palace, and Parliament House, and of the High Church and ancient dwellings grouped about this seat of kings is, indeed, the story of Scottish history.

The field of Bannockburn is within a short drive of Stirling; Bridge of Allan is "over the way"; Keir and Blairdrummond, Airth and Airthrey, and scores of other notable spots are within easy reach by road or rail. Or, if one is bent on a longer excursion, there is another line that penetrates the upper valley of the Forth, skirting the northern slopes of the Gargunnock and Fintry Hills, and opening a connection by the branch line from Bucklyvie to Aberfoyle with the Trossachs, through Strathendrick with Balloch and Loch Lomond, and also through the Blane Valley and under the Campsie Fells, with Glasgow. It traverses regions of Menteith and the Lennox, sorely harried by Rob Roy

LOCH KATRINE AND ELLEN'S ISLE

THE TROSSACHS

and other caterans of the old blackmailing and cattle-lifting days. Kippen, and Bucklyvie, and Drymen, are also names that conjure up many strange and authentic incidents in the annals of the Highland border, and in the family history of the Grahams and Macgregors, the Cumyns and the royal line of Stewart. But here, too, romance and legend have got the upper hand of history, and the spell of Sir Walter Scott is as supreme on the upper waters of the rivers Forth and Teith as on the Tweed.

The branch line from Bucklyvie goes by Gartmore to Aberfoyle, where the plough coulter, wielded by Bailie Nicol Jarvie in Jeanie M'Alpine's change house, is extant, to convince the unbeliever. Loch Ard is near at hand, clothed in copsewood, and overhung by the Crags of Craigmore and Ben Vogrie, and almost under the shadow of Ben Lomond. But greater is the spell of enchantment at the Linn of Ledeart, where Waverley first encountered Flora M'Ivor, then at the Duke Murdoch's Island Castle; at the Fords of Frew, one remembers the parting between Diana Vernon and Francis Osbaldistone more even than the crossing of Prince Charlie's host; and on and around the Lake of Menteith—on Inchmahone, where, under the shelter of the Priory walls and its planes and orchard trees, Mary Stuart spent the quietest and sweetest hours of her childhood, and on the Castle Island where the ancient Lords of Menteith wielded almost regal power—history and tradition, fact and fancy, have become so entwined that they can scarce be disentangled.

For visiting the scenes of "The Lady of the Lake," Loch Katrine and the Trossachs are reached by crossing the hill from Aberfoyle.

As yet, no railway has ventured to invade the enchanted glen up which James Fitzjames spurred his weary horse in pursuit of the stag, and down which, after many adventures, he followed Roderick Dhu to the place of combat at Coilantogle Ford. But a fine coach road winds by Vennacher and Achray and through the Pass of the Trossachs, and opens up this "fastness of the North" to all and sundry; the route is well "plenished" with hotels and other places of entertainment for the traveller; there is a steamer on Loch Katrine for those who would scan "Ellen's Isle" more closely, or would pass on by Stronachlacher, at the head of the loch, to the shores of Loch Lomond. "Dark Roderick" might think the scene strangely and sadly changed, and might resent this invasion, by the Sassenach, of this last sanctuary of his proscribed clan. But the spell that keeps drawing the tourist host hither has given a new lustre and meaning to every name in the valley—to Duncraggan and Brig o' Turk, to "lone Glenfinlas" and "dark Glengyle." Ben An's "forehead bare" and the craggy front of "huge Ben Venue" have never looked the same since they were touched by the wizard's wand; and the charm that the visitor finds in every green nook and cranny, every glimpse of copsewood and tumbling water, moss-grown bent and lichened rock, the charm that is most potent by the "Silver Strand," or

> "Where twines the path, in shadow hid,
> Round many a rocky pyramid,"

has been in part evoked by the touches of the "Harp of the North."

To Fife and the North.

THERE is a nearer and a more direct way from the Waverley Station to where Perth—"Bonnie Saint Johnstoun"—stands fair upon Tay and marshals the holiday-making crowds bound for the central Highlands. This is by the Forth Bridge, at which we have already glanced more than once. It is the successful solution of a problem in bridge-building that had baffled many inventive minds, and is one of the greatest triumphs of railway engineering. It has brought Perth within an hour's ride of the Waverley, and since it was opened for traffic, in March 1890, the traveller has been enabled with the help of its complement, the Tay Bridge, to step down at Aberdeen four hours after leaving Edinburgh, having skimmed over two broad firths on his way.

Figures have been accumulated to give an idea of the gigantic character of the enterprise, from an engineering point of view. It is upwards of one and a-half miles in length, fully two-thirds of which is over salt water; the great central arches, resting on Inchgarvie, are nearly a third of a mile in span; the summits of the great cantilever piers rise to a height of 361 feet above high-water; 50,000 tons of steel have been used in the structure, and the surface requiring to be painted covers no less than 120 acres. The Bridge took seven years in building. It is, however, the lightness not the mass of the Bridge that takes the eye of the beholder; it is like a gossamer web spun across the narrows; yet its enormous strength has already been tested and proved in a hundred gales. And the view from it, as much as the appearance of the wonderful structure itself, is impressed on the traveller's mind, as he seems to hang in air over the two Queensferrys and over the waters of the Firth, spreading eastwards between curving shores and among many islands, towards the open sea, and tapering, like a sword blade, towards the west and the heart of the Highlands. Then he plunges with the train into Fife.

The North British Railway has covered Fife with its ramifications. By means of it one visits the long array of quaint Fife burghs and fishing havens—beloved of the wandering artist, and haunted by memories and traditions of the olden time —that are hemmed on the fringes of the " Kingdom," from Kincardine round the East Neuk to St Andrews, and back along the shores of the Tay to Newburgh; its breezy and spacious golf links, and its stretches of bathing sands, its caves and standing-stones, and its ancient castles and churches nodding over the salt water. Nor are legends and relics of the past less rife in the interior of Fife, at the foot of the Lomonds and the Ochils, around Loch Leven, and in the valley of the Eden.

An example of the historic Fife burgh is met with as we emerge from the tunnel beyond the Forth Bridge, in Inverkeithing, seated on its sheltered but shallow bay; and within sight is Rosyth Castle, a surf-beaten tower that belonged to a Stewart family, from which Cromwell is said to have drawn his ancestry. The Protector won his great victory on the hillsides beyond; we pass the battlefield if our route be Perthwards, and come to Dunfermline, the old seat of Kings, where Canmore welcomed his saint and queen, after whom St Margaret's Hope and Queensferry are named, and where the royal pair are buried, along with Robert the Bruce and other famous and princely personages, at the East .end of the grand old Abbey Church. Little is left of the tower in Pittencrieff Glen in which, in the ballad of Sir Patrick Spens, the King sat "drinking the blood-red wine." But there are considerable remains of the later Palace, in which Charles I. and the Electress Palatine were born. For the rest, is not Dr Andrew Carnegie a native of Dunfermline, and is not the place, which does a large trade in linen manufactures, the recipient of his benefactions, in the shape of Town Hall, Baths, and so forth?

The next place of note reached is Kinross, on the margin of Loch Leven, an anglers' paradise, which mirrors the Lomond and Navity hills, and surrounds St Serf's Inch and the island prison from which Mary Stuart escaped to a worse fate. The pastoral Ochils are crossed, and through the winding and wooded gorge of Glenfarg we descend, passing at no great distance Abernethy, the old Pictish capital, and its round tower, to Pitkeathly Wells and the Bridge of Earn,

where we bore through the Hill of Moncrieffe, and come to the light of day beside the South Inch of Perth.

At this "Charing Cross of the Highlands,"—so beautiful for situation, so famous in legend and in national annals—the scene of the Combat on the Inch, of the Tragedy in the Blackfriars, of the Gowrie Conspiracy—we have choice of ways for exploring the region beyond.

But the "middle way"—the Highland line—has the strongest attractions. After passing, on the other side of the noble Tay, historic Scone, it follows the main valley of the grandest of Scottish rivers, past Birnam Wood and Dunkeld Cathedral. From Ballinluig you may continue up the Tay to Aberfeldy, and thence, on wheels or on foot, trace it to Kenmore and its gathering basin in Loch Tay, and explore the beauties of Glenlyon and other great valleys of

PERTH

Breadalbane under the shadow of Ben Lawers. Or, keeping the main line, you can follow up the Tummel to Pitlochrie, whence a coach route diverges towards Rannoch under the pyramid of Schiehallion; and accompany the roaring Garry through the Pass of Killiecrankie and over the field of Dundee's victory and fall, to Blair Athol and Struan. Thence, leaving pinewood and precipice behind, you pursue the route over wild moorland, across which one may catch glimpses of snow-streaked Grampian peaks and sullen lochs, to the Pass of Drumouchter and over the water-shed into the valley of the Spey. The bare solitudes of Badenoch, tenanted only by grouse and sheep and deer, give place to the richer beauties of Strathspey, a country of rock and wood and water, dominated by the soaring blue masses of the Cairngorms; we pass Kingussie and Kincraig,

Ruthven Castle, Loch Inch and Kinrara Hill; and, if we are not following the "Highland Spey" down to Grantown and Craigellachie, or making for Forres by Castle Grant and the Findhorn woods, from Aviemore we cut athwart the valley of the Dulnan, Strathdearn and Strathnairn, and cross Culloden Moor to Inverness.

At the "Capital of the Highlands" one is at the heart of everything, if the purpose be to explore, by land or water, the more northerly parts of the country of "Bens and Glens and Heroes." The Ness and the Canal open, from Inverness, the Great Caledonian Glen; by rail, by road, and by sea there are accesses to both sides of the Moray Firth—to Nairn, Forres, Elgin and Aberdeen

INVERNESS

to the east, and to Dingwall and Tain, Thurso and Wick to the north. One can hold on past Inverness almost to the farthest verge of the Scottish mainland. One can also turn aside by the way, at Beauly, to explore Strathglass and its tributary glens of Affric, Cannich, and the rest—a lovely and almost unvisited lake and mountain region; at Muir of Ord, to examine the "Black Isle," the remains of the Cathedral of Ross at Fortrose and Rosemarkie, and the "Hugh Miller country" around Cromarty; at Dingwall to ascend Ben Wyvis, take the waters of Strathpeffer Spa, and cross Ross-shire to the shores of Loch Carron and the Kyle of Loch Alsh; at Bonar Bridge to make acquaintance with Dornoch and its golf links, or to penetrate the recesses of Strathoykell; or at Golspie to visit Dunrobin Castle. Or from Wick or Thurso one can make one's way to John o' Groats and the Pentland tides; or take voyage for the Orkneys and the "furthest Thule" of Shetland.

TO ABERDEEN BY THE TAY BRIDGE.

BUT to return to Fife, and to Inverkeithing. Here another great main road of commerce and travel turns eastward for a little way along the southern fringe of the "Kingdom," and passing through Burntisland and Kirkcaldy strikes across by way of the county town of Cupar to the Tay Bridge and Dundee, and thence keeps as a rule close to the coast, by Arbroath, Montrose and Stonehaven, to Aberdeen. On this, as on the other route, there are many temptations, and also opportunities, to halt by the way or to turn aside from the track. In traversing Fife, for example, one comes first to Aberdour, with the old castle of Regent Morton overtopping the station, with its sheltered bay and "silver sand," and with Inchcolm and its Abbey in the offing. Beyond, after skirting the Hawes Wood and the sea, after passing Burntisland, with the Bin impending over the town, and Rossend Castle—scene of Queen Mary's adventure with Chastelard—overlooking its busy docks and coal wharves, one comes to ancient Kinghorn, at the point of the rocky ridge, over which Alexander III. stumbled to his death, that commands the seaway between it and Inchkeith. At Kirkcaldy, fronted by a bay on which the ruined towers of Seafield and Ravenscraig stand as sentinels, and backed by the woods of Raith, the line turns inland, leaving the floor-cloth factories of the "Lang toun," and Dysart, with its rock-hewn harbour and its tower of St Serf's on the sea-marge, for country scenes dominated by the twin Lomonds.

From Thornton you can diverge through the Fife coalfield to Dunfermline; or to the coal-shipping port of Methil, past the sculptured caves of Wemyss, the castle of the "Thane of Fife," and fish-scented Buckhaven. Or, better still, one can take the route which fetches a compass round the East Neuk to St Andrews, halting, as you have a mind, at Leven or Lundin, for exercise on the thymy golf links; at the little "Robinson Crusoe's harbour," under Largo Law; at the sea-bathing and golfing resort of Elie; at St Monance, whose fishing Haven and venerable fourteenth-century Church are places of pilgrimage for the artist; at time-worn Pittenweem, with its ruined Priory looking across to the "mother-house" on the May and to the Bass; at the "Ansters" and Nether Kilrenny, important fishery stations once celebrated for their fairs and kirk broils; and at Crail, the quaintest and most old fashioned—Culross perhaps excepted—of the little seaports of Fife.

Resuming the main traverse of Fife, one can turn aside at Markinch for Leslie, or from Ladybank can join the Perth line, either through Auchtermuchty and the "Howe of Fife," or by the crumbling remains of Lindores Abbey, "Macduff's Cross," and the town of Newburgh. On the way to "Cupar-in-Fife" —another place of history and legend, as becomes the capital of a historic shire— one passes not far from Falkland Palace, the hunting-seat and favourite country resort of a succession of Scottish kings, within whose walls—recently restored to something of their former splendour by the late Lord Bute—David, Duke of Rothesay, met a mysterious fate at the hands of his uncle, Albany. From

TAY BRIDGE

Leuchars, a place halfway between Cupar and the Fife end of the Tay Bridge, and the possessor of an interesting old Norman church, one most readily reaches St Andrews, the little "grey city by the sea"—the former seat of the Scottish Primacy, the modern shrine and home of golf. Its grim Castle, which witnessed Cardinal Beaton's murder; its tower of St Rule's, almost all that is left of the once magnificent Cathedral; its Town Church, where Knox and Melville preached; its College courts; its old streets and "pends"; its links and sands and rocky shores have gathered about them a crowd of memories, historic and literary, which it would take many pages to rehearse.

The new Tay Bridge is a structure which comes only second to the Forth Bridge among undertakings of its kind in Scotland. Beside it, like stepping-stones across the Firth, are the piers of its predecessor. The lattice-girders and steel floor are carried on double-shafted iron piers, connected by an arch at the top, and resting on a bed of masonry, built above high-water level, over cylinders filled with brick and mortar. Eighty-five spans in all connect the two shores nearly two miles apart; the height of the under side of the girders above high water is seventy-seven feet. It drops the traveller into the heart of the busy city of Dundee, a place of trade and enterprise, with its iron foundries and jute and other manufactures, and also a large shipping and shipbuilding trade. But it has antiquities left in the old Town Steeple and Town Cross, in the "Howff" and the Cowgate, and in the neighbouring Dudhope Tower, the birthplace of "Bonnie Dundee"; and its interest in art and education is attested by such buildings as the Albert Institute and University College. At Broughty Ferry is the old fortified Keep, the guardian of the Tay; and beyond it opens a great expanse of bent and turf and sandhills, occupied as military camping and exercise ground and shooting ranges; while as golf links Monifieth and

ABERDEEN

Carnoustie rival the famous greens of Fife and East Lothian. Arbroath boasts of its shore scenery and of the fine fragments of its Tyronesian Abbey as well as its commercial energy; and beyond Auchmithie—the "Musselcrag" of "The Antiquary"—and the grand, solitary sweep of Lunan Bay, the line crosses the Esk, and traverses the peninsula between its shallow estuary and the sea, on which is picturesquely planted the town of Montrose.

Here, too, notable events have happened and notable men have lived in the past; and here, too, there are golf links and bathing ground, held in great esteem by those happy enough to know them and Montrose. There is rail connection with Bervie, along the coast; with the old Cathedral town of Brechin, and with Edzell, in the old Lindsay country, set far into the Braes of Angus. The main line, in the meantime, leaves the sea, to make a detour through the "Howe of the Mearns," by Laurencekirk and Fordoun, and after passing Monboddo and Drumtochtie's Glen, to rejoin it at bracing and pleasant Stonehaven. Again the line skirts the edges of coast precipices, hollowed into fantastic shapes by the waves; again the traveller notes with interest a fisher haven sheltering in a quiet creek, or a handful of lichened gravestones, and the gable of a little ruined church leaning towards the cliff edge and the sea. Dunnottar Castle—

BALMORAL

where the Scottish Regalia was sent for safety in troublous times, and where the "Martyrs of the Covenant" were pent, whose record has been kept legible by the chisel of "Old Mortality" in the parish churchyard—looms out on one dark promontory; Findon, once famous for its "haddies," is perched on another. Then come Nigg Bay and Girdleness, the Dee and Aberdeen.

The "Granite City" has grown and thriven greatly of late years, until it is almost abreast of Dundee in population, and has spread over the space between Dee and Don. It is surrounding and invading the cloistral calm that once brooded over Old Aberdeen, with its venerable King's College and St Machar's Cathedral, and reaching near to the "Brig of Balgownie." It is a place of commerce and shipping, with spacious docks and harbour, and the centre of a fish trade that yields precedence only to Grimsby. But still more proud is Aberdeen of its noble Union Street and the palaces of white granite that embellish it—of the County Buildings; of the great Church of St Nicholas, re-erected after destruction by fire; and of the Mitchell Hall of the united King's and Marischal Colleges. It upholds its reputation for learning and art as well as for hardheaded business qualities, and does not forget the days of old when it withstood in arms the Lord of the Isles, the Marquis of Montrose, and the "Gordons of the North."

From Aberdeen the way to Inverness holds on, through an important agricultural region, round "the back of Bennachie," to Grange and Keith, where alternative routes can be chosen, by the Banffshire coast, by Mulben, and by Craigellachie, that converge upon Elgin. There are branch lines that ascend the valley of the Don, or penetrate to Macduff and Banff, to the great seats of the herring fishery, Fraserburgh and Peterhead, or to Cruden and its golf links and the "Bullers of Buchan." But in Deeside, perhaps, lies the chief magnet of the tourists who pour into Aberdeen station. In that quarter are to be found Banchory, Aboyne, and Ballater; Glentanar, Glenmuick and Glengairn; Abergeldie and the Kirk of Crathie; Braemar and the Linn of Dee, and paths leading to the crests of Ben Macdhuie and Lochnagar; above all, there is Balmoral.

GLASGOW AND THE WEST.

FROM the Waverley Station, Glasgow is distant little more than an hour. One of the pleasantest methods of making acquaintance with the populous city on the Clyde, is to make short descents upon it from Edinburgh. The direct line is by Polmont and Lenzie to Queen Street. The route is through the great central depression of Scotland, between the valleys of Forth and Clyde, parallel to the Canal and to the Wall of Antonine, traces of which may be seen from the train in the neighbourhood of Bonnybridge and Castlecary. The Kilsyth and Campsie Hills loom up to the north; and to these inviting slopes there is access by Kirkintilloch, over part of the oldest rail track of the North British system. Less speedy, but not without attractions of its own, is the line that opens up the shale oil fields of Uphall and Broxburn and Bathgate, and the "Black Country" of Airdrie and Coatbridge, whence a branch runs through the moorish region of New Monkland and Slamannan, while another extends across the Clyde to Hamilton, passing the stream between Bothwell Castle and Bothwell Bridge, and conducting almost to the gates of the Palace in which is housed what is left of the Duke of Hamilton's art treasures.

The Bathgate line also lands the passenger in the heart of the city. He steps out of the station into George Square, and finds Glasgow's monuments ranked around him, and the Municipal Buildings reared above. Argyll Street, Buchanan Street and Sauchiehall Street are close at hand. The Broomielaw and the Clyde Bridges and shipping; the Saltmarket, the Green, and St Mungo's Cathedral are not far off. There are many and easy routes for reaching the Art Galleries and the Botanic Gardens on the Kelvin, the University on Gilmorehill, the shipbuilding yards of Govan and Partick, Yoker and Clydebank, and the hundred other places in and around "the second city of the Empire" that invite a visit.

From Glasgow ways open up, by river and land, to all parts of the West —to Upper Clydesdale, to the "Land of Burns," to Paisley, Greenock, and the infinite number of holiday resorts embraced in the local phrase "doun the water." But the route which the traveller, who makes Edinburgh and the North British Station Hotel his headquarters, may well prefer above all others is that which, from Cowlairs, skirts the northern suburbs of Glasgow, and slipping past the Kilpatrick hills at Bowling, presently brings him under the towering mass of Dumbarton Rock.

The lofty, isolated double-headed crag stands sentinel at once over the channel of the Clyde and over the valley of the Leven. For a thousand years it was the defence of kings; to Dumbarton Castle, Wallace was taken a prisoner, and in it Mary Stuart, a child of six, found refuge before taking flight to France. In these days a busy town, with a great shipbuilding trade and turkey-red manufactures, is grouped at the base of the Rock, which is washed on one side by the stately Firth of Clyde and on the other by the waters that issue out of Loch Lomond. By the leafy Leven valley—by the line that runs by Renton and Alexandria and Tobias Smollett's old home of Bonhill, to Balloch pier—there is a way leading to the heart of the Highlands. The graceful pyramid of Ben Lomond, buttressed by Ptarmigan, presides over the scene—over the loch and its many wooded islands; over the country of the Grahams, of the Colquhouns, and of the "Wild Macgregors" on both banks; over Strathendrick and Buchanan Castle; over Luss and Glenfruin; over the Pass of Balmaha and the Falls of Inversnaid.

From the pier of Craigendoran, reached after passing Dumbarton and Cardross, lines of steamers take their departure for Greenock pier across the Firth; for Dunoon and Kirn, Rothesay and Brodick, Ardrishaig and Inveraray, and a host of other far-famed watering-places on the lower Clyde. Helensburgh, close by, is one of the most handsome and favoured of these holiday resorts; and all round the shores of the Gareloch, upon which the passenger by the West Highland Railway looks down from his vantage ground situated high up the engirdling hillsides, are scattered charming nooks — Row, Shandon, and, on the further side of the Loch, Roseneath

LOCH LOMOND

and Baremman—where the tired sojourners in the city gladly recruit their energies in the air from the hills and from the sea.

THE WEST HIGHLAND RAILWAY.

SINCE the opening, in 1894, of the West Highland Railway, as part of the North British system, there is access by another route to Loch Lomond and "Rob Roy's Country," and to fine mountain, moor and loch scenery lying much farther afield. It begins at Craigendoran at the mouth of the Gareloch, and stretches to Fort William and Banavie, at the head of Loch Linnhe, whence an extension is carried through a glorious Highland region—Lochiel's and Clanranald's country, and the scenes of Prince Charlie's landings and wanderings —to Mallaig on the Sound of Skye.

OBAN

When the isthmus between Garelochhead and Loch Long is passed at Whistlefield, wilder scenes break on the view. Human dwellings are still rare on the middle and upper reaches of Loch Long; but mountains abound, and the tumbled confusion of ridges and corries of "Argyll's Bowling Green," and the broken crown of Ben Arthur or "The Cobbler," make a magnificent western sky line. Presently, the precipitous jaws of Glencroe open up, leading by "Rest and be Thankful" to Loch Fyne and Inveraray; and from Arrochar at the head of Loch Long, the line crosses over to Tarbet, on Loch Lomond — from the salt water to the fresh. Ben Lomond is almost opposite, and Inversnaid and Rob Roy's Cave and the road to the Trossachs are not far ahead across the narrowing lake, along whose margin, among pinewood and oak and birch coppice, bracken and heather and boulders, the track winds to Ardlui, where the Falloch pours in at the northern extremity of the "Queen of Scottish Lochs." Thence the way is through the green fields, past the storm-stressed ancient firs, and along the heathy hillsides of Glenfalloch, hemmed in by great rock ramparts, Ben Cabhair and his marrows, and accompanied by the "sound of many waters," until the descent is made to Crianlarich, the crossing-place of the Callander and Oban line.

This lonely railway cross-roads, at the head of Glen Dochart, has some majestic neighbours. For Ben Lui on the west, and Ben More and Stobinian on the east, with other heights rising near to the 4,000 feet line, look down upon it, tempting the active mountaineer to ascents, and filling up pleasantly the waiting-time at Crianlarich platform that is spent in noting their peaks and corries. At Crianlarich, passengers for Oban, &c., pass on to the Callander and Oban Railway.

Striding across the rival line and the Fillan, the West Highland creeps below the knees of Ben Chaluim and Ben Odhar to "the fountains of the Tay,"

85

GLENCOE

passing St Fillan's Chapel and Dalrigh—the
"King's˙ Field"—where the Brooch of Lorn
was reft from the Bruce, on the day when

"Rung aloud Ben Dourish fell,
 Answered Dochart's sounding dell,
 Fled the deer from wild Tyndrum,
 When the homicide, o'ercome,
 Hardly 'scaped with scaith and scorn,
 Left the pledge with conquering Lorn."

At "wild Tyndrum" the two lines, which have kept near to each other and almost
parallel, part company, the one striking off through Glen Lochay for Dalmally, and
the West Highland holding north into the upper valley of the Orchy, round the
roots of "beautiful Ben Dorein," so sweetly sung by the Highland Bard, Duncan
Ban Macintyre, and past Loch Tulla. Here the lofty peaks of the Black Mount,
green on their lower slopes, craggy on their summits, and riven by the deep gashes
of thunderstorms, seem to rise straight up from the rail track at a slope which
only goats could climb. To the west are the great shapes of Ben Cruachan,
Clachlet, Buchail Etive, and the mountains of Glencoe, into which fateful gorge
the turnpike leads away across Orchy Bridge and by Kingshouse Inn.

Once more the scene changes when the line ascends into the black
wilderness of peat bog of the desolate Moor of Rannoch, through which the
lazy Ghaoir wanders from one marshy lochan to another on its way to Loch
Rannoch. There is yet another change when, "long, sinuous, black, dreary
Acharon-like" Loch Lydoch and the Black Water being left behind, one comes
to Loch Ossian and Loch Treig and the sources of the Spean. For we are
now in the wilds of Lochaber. Ben Alder, where Prince Charlie — and
David Balfour—sought refuge with Cluny in the "Cage," looms up at the
head of a glen to the east, and the tremendous precipices with which Ben
Nevis fronts the sun tower up against the western sky. The Treig is followed

to the Spean at Inverlair, and the Spean to Roy Bridge, below the famous
" Parallel Roads," and the scene of the last of the " Clan battles," where " Coll
of the Cows " defeated the Mackintoshes ; and then comes Spean Bridge, from which
a new branch line, as yet unopened for traffic, traverses the Great Caledonian
Glen, by Loch Lochy and Loch Oich, and the side of the Canal to Fort
Augustus and Loch Ness.

The main line of the West Highland keeps bending round the outer skirts
of Ben Nevis, whose huge bulk more and more asserts itself as the monarch of
the scene, until at Lochy Bridge, overlooking Inverlochy Castle, old and new,
and the scene of Montrose's victory over Argyll, we are at the very base
of the highest of Scottish mountains, and close to the pony track that leads to
the Observatory on its summit. Fort William, a growing tourist centre, is
reached as soon as we cross the Nevis, rushing down through its wild glen ;
and, by a loop line crossing the Lochy, Corpach Moss, and the Caledonian
Canal, we come to Banavie.

The Mallaig Extension.

BANAVIE and Fort William are at the confluence of the land and water
carriage of the north-west Highlands. They are the halfway houses on
the voyage by steamer between Oban and Inverness ; and there passengers
step on board or disembark who are bound to or from Foyers and Invergarry,
Ballachulish and Glencoe, Appin and Ardgour, Mull and the Outer Isles. But
to reach the western shores of Inverness and Ross, and the outlying Hebrides,
it had been necessary to make a long detour to the north or south, round by
Ben Wyvis, or through the Sound of Mull ; or, if they journeyed in a more
direct route overland, it had to be by slow and costly coach stages, or on foot.
Passengers from the south, on business or pleasure bent, could not reach
Glen Finnan or Moidart, Skye or the Lews, without spending a night or nights

MALLAIG

by the way; and the fish and other produce of those regions of the west, took as long, or longer, to find the way to market.

The West Highland Railway, with its Mallaig extension, has changed all that. The traveller who leaves the Waverley Station in the early morning is on the shore of Morar, on the lip of Loch Nevis and opposite to the Point of Sleat and the Coolins, before midday; he is in Portree early in the afternoon, and in Stornoway Bay the same evening. On his overland journey he has traversed a region of the Highlands that keeps growing in scenic beauty and in legendary interest as he proceeds.

After leaving Banavie and the Canal, the line holds along the northern shore of the sea arm of Loch Eil, past Kilmallie Kirk and Fassfern, and then up the Finlay Glen and down the Callop to Loch Shiel. This is the route taken on many a "spreach" of the Cameron and Clanranald men, and it is the road that was followed by Prince Charlie's Highlanders, after they had raised the standard of the Stuarts in Glen Finnan. The memorable spot is marked by a monument on the flat

PRINCE CHARLIE'S MONUMENT, LOCH SHIEL, GLEN FINNAN

haugh at the head of the Loch, near where a fine viaduct carries the railway across the Finnan; and opposite is the tiny island where Saint Finnan and other missionary monks from Iona first planted the cross in this wild territory.

The country grows still wilder and more beautiful further on, as we trace the shores of Loch Eilt, and descend to the rocky and bosky fringes of the salt water at the head of Loch Ailort and of Loch-nan-Uamh, the scene of the lawless exploits of Donald Balloch, and Allan-nan-Corc. Here are the woods and caves of Borrowdale, in which the Prince sought refuge again and again from his pursuers; the strand on which he first set foot on the Scottish mainland on the 26th July, 1745, and whence, a year later, he re-embarked for France after twelve months more crowded with strange adventures, and with proofs of loyal devotion, than are to be met with in the tale of any paladin of romance.

From Arisaig we look out across Atlantic waters to the great headland of Ardnamurchan, to Scuir-Eigg, and to the mountains of Rum and of Skye.

Tourists are sure to discover this nook in the West, where the breezes are so mild as well as so fresh and healthful; where the sea is strewn with islands, and margined with coppice and wild flowers, and where along with lovely scenery there is the air of romance. The line does not end at this favoured and beautiful spot, but stretches northward under the caves and corries of Craig More, and across peat mosses to the hills and streams of Morar.

A tumultuous stream rushes down in its short mile course from the Loch to the sea, dividing South from North Morar; and where the banks are prettiest and the river wildest, it is crossed by the railway bridge. The "Prince" once took shelter in a bothy hard by, and after "supping on cold salmon," hid his head for the night in a cave in the cliff face by the river side. The hills around the head of Loch Morar were also his hiding-place. The Loch itself is said to be the deepest fresh water lake in Britain, and local tradition tells of a huge monster that lurks in its abysses, and shows himself from time to time when misfortune

ARISAIG FROM THE LOCH

is at hand. Truer is the tale of how that hoary sinner, Simon Fraser, Lord Lovat, hid for weeks on an island of the Loch, and escaped in a boat—for a time—from the red-coated hunters.

North Morar—the "Blessed Morar" of the West Highland Catholics, for here the "heather priests" were reared and taught, and suffered persecution—is traversed to Mallaig; and still we are on the traces of the "yellow-haired laddie." He landed in Mallaig harbour, almost on the spot where the West Highland Railway has its terminus, after his weary wanderings in Skye and Knoydart; and he "slept for three nights in the open air," not far from where Mallaig Hotel offers handsome entertainment to its guests. To the Mallaig of to-day is sent the harvest of the sea from the Outer Isles on its way to the Southern markets; and from its pier the steamers transport the tourist crowds to the Kyle of Lochalsh, to Broadford and Portree, to Gairloch and Ullapool, to Stornoway and the furthest Hebrides. There is nothing to prevent it becoming another Oban.

PRINCES STREET

North British Hotel and North Bridge.

THE NEW EDINBURGH

LD habits die hard. As the 1990s opened the Edinburgh Balmoral emerged from the scaffolding chrysalis which wrapped up the North British, but it will be a long time before local people forget to call it the "NB".

The harsh fact is that the new name was not chosen for the sake of local people any more than the old one was. Thousands of visitors arriving in Edinburgh from all over the world will not think twice about it: they are looking for somewhere comfortable and recognisably Scottish right in the centre of the capital city. The new name marked a change of identity and, with a fascinating twist of fate, the ten storey building at the east end of Princes Street once more became the flagship of a growing business empire. The hotel reopened with a pioneering spirit which echoed the original opening of the North British almost 90 years ago.

Then it was a curiously low-key affair. On Wednesday 15 October 1902 a small advertisement appeared on the front page of the *Scotsman*:

"North British Station Hotel

This hotel in direct communication with Waverley Station is now open

F.T. Burcher, hotel manager."

That was all. On the Edinburgh Stock Market North British Railway shares dropped 1s 3d and two days later rose by 17s 6d. Otherwise the city does not seem to have paid undue attention to its precocious new landmark, the only residential building ever erected on the south side of Princes Street. The Lord Provost's Committee had even turned down the architect's request for a marquee in front of the entrance hall.

But that hardly mattered. The opening of the hotel was advertised not only in the Scotsman but in newspapers and journals across Europe and beyond. The North British Hotel was a vanguard for the railway company which built it, a surrogate for the grand station they had never been permitted to erect in the sensitive site between Old and New Town. The name itself symbolises such driving ambition.

The term "North British" was a curious snobbery left over from the early days of the union which bound Scotland and England into a United Kingdom. The "best" families had headed notepaper marking their address as North Britain, not Scotland, and in choosing the name the railway company deliberately selected their clientele, seeing Edinburgh not just as a provincial capital but as the centre of a much larger world.

You can see that extraordinary sense of confidence and competition in the building itself. Now it has been restored to the original golden sandstone it is a bold ebullient place, bursting with towers and balconies and topped with a crown. A pugnacious building firmly planting a mixture of European styles — French Renaissance, Dutch dormers — right in the middle of the Scottish capital where, when it opened, cows were still milked in the closes of the old High Street just a few yards across North Bridge. With the paradoxical juxtaposition of progress, the poor died of cholera in overcrowded slums within sniffing distance of the palatial bathrooms of the grand cosmopolitan hotel. But the North British was a sign of the future heralded by the railways, the newly opened Forth Bridge and the electric lights switched on in Princes Street just seven years earlier.

A CIRCUS ON NORTH BRIDGE: THE HOTEL UNDER CONSTRUCTION IN THE BACKGROUND

Growing prosperity was celebrated in the number of important organisations which liked to be seen celebrating at the North British Hotel. While international celebrities arrived at Waverley Station, local VIPs went in through the front door. Anyone who was anyone automatically went to the hotel which could cope with dinner for 450. The Cockburn Association, which had been horrified by the general bad taste of the building, came to accept it as a "friendly monster". The North British clock acted as a focal point for generations of the hurrying public and by tradition was kept a few minutes fast to give them time to catch their trains.

As a railway hotel the North British settled down for a long comfortable reputation of being taken for granted: part of the city scenery.

ROOTS IN THE RAILWAY

To see how deep the hotel roots lie in Waverley Station you have only to stand at Platform 19 where trains leave on the hour for Kings Cross, London. The journey time has almost halved — from eight hours to four-and-a-half — steam has given way to electricity and trains now compete with aircraft and the motor car rather than (as yet anyway) a rival railway service. But in the arches of the station wall you can still see the place where trains delivered coal to feed the insatiable boilers of the hotel. In return, from the same standpoint the boilers pumped steam to start the heaters of the sleeper carriages. The railway brought people and provisions and the hotel fed and watered the trains in a partnership of mutual dependence which was to last 80 years.

Long before the North British Railway Company began blasting into the wall of rock behind Waverley Station, however, a warning was issued to shareholders. "Large hotel traffic does not mean profit," wrote D. Hill Murray to the Evening News in 1885, "the hotel will be constructed in most sumptuous manner regardless of cost to shareholders." Besides, he pointed out, "The Caledonian have a much better site and they will follow suit."

Both statements proved to be prophetic. No expense was spared in creating the new hotel and it would be a long time before the flow of 40,000 visitors each year even covered the costs of running a construction which devoured coal and coke by up to 200 tons a month. But Mr Murray had missed the real point. The North British Station Hotel was never intended to be merely a hotel, it was to be a monument to the railway company, the grand eye-catching "station" they had never been permitted to build above ground. It would be their equivalent of the St Pancras or York Central Station that the ancient laws of Edinburgh had never allowed them to build in the sensitive Waverley site within view of the powerful Governor and Directors of the Bank of Scotland on the Mound. Every time a signal box or office reared its ugly head 30 feet above ground level the Bank ordered it to be removed.

So the hotel, strategically situated out of the Bank's firing line, was a physical and political achievement. What's more the NBR beat the Caledonian to it — the rival hotel opened at the other end of Princes Street in 1903 and even now the sense of rivalry lingers, a legacy of fierce competition between two railway companies who sometimes literally shoved each other off the line in the determination to get there first.

George Wieland was the man who saw the potential of a hotel in Princes

Street. An NBR company secretary who "retired" to the board in 1890, Wieland threw himself into developing what was then called the Waverley Station Hotel — not just for the capital of Scotland but as the centre of a European network.

Hence the advertisements placed not only in the *Scotsman,* but in the *Daily Telegraph,* London, the *New York Herald, Figaro* in Paris and *Cavio* in Egypt. Hence the grand tour of the best hotels in Europe before the architect W. Hamilton Beattie even submitted his first linen-bound, water-coloured plans to Edinburgh Corporation. First Wieland went to see the Metropole Hotel in Brighton then, in 1895, led his hotel committee on a grand tour of the great hotels of Europe. After staying at the Hamburgher Hof in Hamburg, the Central, Savoy and Bristol in Berlin, the Imperial and Bristol in Vienna, the Hotel Hungaria and the Royal in Budapest as well others in Paris, Amsterdam and Brussels, the committee reported back "no improvement on hotels in this country" and kitchens far inferior to the newest in Edinburgh. What Wieland learned from the tour, however, was the importance of grand banqueting halls to bring winter business. Generations of Edinburgh civic functions, balls and weddings have proved him right.

SOPHIA LOREN: STARS COULD SHINE OR REMAIN UNSEEN

As Mr Murray had feared the hotel was to be a sumptuous place, but he could not have predicted the enormous range of expenses — from lighting (and winding) the clock to advertising in railway carriages. There were some economies: Professor Barr from Glasgow University designed the electrical system so that only one light at a time would go on in the bedrooms no matter how many switches were pressed.

The Caledonian was always breathing down Wieland's neck. He set himself a four year task of stocking the hotel cellars with the best of champagne, hocks, ports and whiskey, reporting regularly to the committee on his progress with the ever present goal that "30,000 to 40,000 quarts of champagne are said to be used annually in the Caledonian Company's Central Station Hotel in Glasgow."

Ironically for both Caledonian and North British Railway Companies by far the greatest publicity went to the opening of a different building. The City Hospital, opened by King Edward VII in May 1903, was a great symbol of progress in a city where, no more than five minutes walk from the North British, people lived in squalor and died from disease. Almost half the city population lived in two room flats and were lucky if they shared a water closet on the stair landing. But the

North British with 300 bedrooms, 52 bathrooms and 70 lavatories and a constant circulation of fresh air was aimed instead at wealthy landed families who were constantly on the move between summer and winter residences, taking whole households as they went.

Hotel porters in red jackets met guests off the train and took them by lift direct from station booking hall to a reception desk in the basement of the hotel. Another lift whisked them up to the entrance hall, the Palm Court and beyond to the bedrooms. For guests: bedrooms furnished in mahogany, leather and crimson moquette. For their servants: walnut upholstered in hair and hardcloth.

The soothing rhythms of Edwardian society are recorded in old hotel leaflets and leather bound statements of accounts. In a world of well-ordered priorities the bill for plants and flowers exceeded that for gas, travelling salesmen were entertained in the "Commercial" lounge and billiards and smoking rooms were placed at a discreet distance to avoid discomfort to ladies. The minutiae listed in the inventory of furnishings is awesome, from japanned dishes to catch drips from fire hydrants to bath thermometers in lacquered cases, from satin bed covers to white cotton gloves for staff, from pincushions to a silver burnishing machine. And for whose use were the 24 enamelled spittoons?

New Year's 1934

NORTH BRITISH STATION HOTEL, EDINBURGH

LNER

DINNER—A la Carte

Hors d'œuvre 2/-
Kidney Soup 1/-

Boiled Tripe and Onion Sauce 3/-
Irish Stew 3/-
Filleted Turbot Duglere 3/-
Roasted or Boiled Potatoes 6d
Spinach in Cream 1/-

Greengage Tart 1/-
Mince Pies 1/-
Vanilla Ice 1/-

28th December 1946.

Under the Meals in Establishments Order 1946, bread can only be served as one of the three permissible courses, and can only be served on request.
A service charge of 10 per cent is added to all bills, and covers all services in this Hotel.

MENUS TELL THE STORY OF THE TIMES: A TOUCH OF ART NOUVEAU DECADENCE FROM 1934; BUT TRIPE ON THE MENU DURING THE POST-WAR AUSTERITY

Not surprisingly years passed before the hotel and grill room made a profit, despite enough visitors to keep busy two reception desks. But the year before the Great War, from £64,084 4s 7d of "business done" and gross profit of £38,641 18s 10d, the hotel recorded net profit of £7,766 4s 6d. In those gilded days guests sat down to menus written entirely in French. On 13 Juillet 1913 the choice included Omelette Paysanne, Quartier d'Agneau Roti and Pouding à la Semoule.

The hotel and railway enjoyed a golden age which was to last until the outbreak of the Second World War. In 1922 the North British Railway Company became part of the London and North Eastern Railway Company and the menus show a stylish modern self-confidence. The hotel bottled and blended its own whisky,

North British Railway Hotel, Edinburgh

THE NORTH BRITISH RAILWAY COMPANY

North British Railway Hotel,

Edinburgh

The Contractors' Dinner, on the occasion of the opening of the Hotel, to be held on Wednesday 15th October, at 6.30 o'clock.

No 58

North British
Railway Hotel,
Edinburgh.

Contractors' Dinner,
15th October 1902,
at 6.30 o'clock.

Admit

THIS PORTION OF THE TICKET
TO BE GIVEN UP ON ENTERING.

No 58

wine and port. "It was a glittering place," says Jackie Monteith who started work as apprentice chef in 1938 at the age of 14. But he returned to a subtly different place after the Second World War. From 1947 the railways were nationalised, the hotel staff became members of the National Union of Railwaymen and the promise of travel was opened to a wider public. The first transatlantic flights landed at Prestwick in 1946, Edinburgh airport opened a new runway in 1970 and as the other side of the world came closer to the city Jackie Monteith remembers a subtle reaction in the hotel kitchen: pineapple replaced peas beside the baked ham.

But the railway connection continued — until the 1980s the kitchens of the hotel were still baking bread and butchering meat for the dining cars down below — and ironically even lorry loads by road had to be delivered via Waverley. The grand old British Transport Hotels were linked with a bond of camaraderie which tied places as different as Turnberry, Leeds and London and still survives their separation from British Rail. Jack Maguire, general manager of the North British from 1979 to 1983, guided the hotel from BTH to its first non-railway owner. Now retired he still meets old friends at the BTH Members Club which bears the motto: "Times change and we with time, but not in ways of friendship." While praising the excellence of BTH training and service Maguire recalls the disadvantage of a central ownership which could never afford to maintain its property. The North British was a very faded "grand old lady" when British Rail sold it in 1983. An era had ended but for the first time in years there was hope of restoring the building to its original grandeur. With some differences. A swimming pool now occupies the second basement where guests once arrived at the station entrance. Direct communication to Waverley has been sealed off. As Jack Maguire puts it with beautiful simplicity: "The umbilical chord has been cut."

A DOUBLE LIFE

But the hotel has always led a double life. When it looked down it saw the railway. When it looked up it surveyed the city.

Cosmopolitan and very much part of home, for the greater part of the 20th century the North British Hotel has been firmly fixed as a city institution. Over the years a regular galaxy of film and sports stars, princesses and politicians, have

THE QUEEN MOTHER: LIKED PLAIN ROAST LAMB FOR LUNCH

posed for photographs by the hotel pillars on Princes Street.

Elizabeth Taylor in cloche hat and dark glasses walked among American visitors in the North British reception hall and no-one spotted she was there. The lobby of a luxury hotel is a fascinatingly bustling place where stars may shine or remain unseen if they prefer. Miss Taylor was quite likely to be outnumbered by guests of thoroughly down to earth organisations from the Scottish Rugby Union, the Chiropodists, High Constables or the Edinburgh Chamber of Commerce. More sensitive international celebrities were ushered discreetly in through the Waverley Steps entrance, but even as they did so local people by the hundred would swing in through the revolving door at the front for balls, banquets and business breakfasts. Jack Maguire says, "Anyone who was anyone living in Edinburgh or visiting the city came to the North British."

The hotel has always been ready to do that bit extra for its guests. In the 1960s an Eastern potentate took over the elegant second floor and had it rearranged so that he could sleep on cushions on the floor with armed guards along the corridors. A mysterious visitor during the Second World War, however, got less favoured treatment. He aroused the suspicions of the head cashier and was arrested as a German spy.

There seems no truth in the legend that a secret passage once connected hotel with Holyrood Palace, the Royal Family's home in Edinburgh ("that would be one hell of a passage" observes Maguire). But for many years until Holyrood accommodation was extended the NB entertained the annual overflow of Royal visitors to the Palace. Jackie Monteith, sauce chef until 1987, remembers the Queen Mother's liking for plain roast lamb for lunch, while the old Princess Royal had her own special dessert: fingers of Madeira cake dipped in egg white rolled in sugar and toasted under the grill.

By the time the hotel closed for refurbishment in 1988 it had become so much part of city life that an interesting group of people met to mark the occasion with a grand breakfast, promising to celebrate the reopening in the same way.

Interesting because in 1902 members of that same vigilant conservation group, the Cockburn Association, were horrified at the way the new hotel completely dominated its surroundings. "Any appreciation of its architecture is neutralised by the sense of disproportion which its height and breadth conveys," was the society's comment at the time. Other critics commented on its aggressive bulk, the bulbous clock tower, "standing at the hinge of Old and New Towns it is coarse and obstructive at once."

PRIME MINISTERS... (EDWARD HEATH)

But times change and familiarity breeds affection. Now the Cockburn Association campaigns for the hotel to become a listed building (if nothing else, it will protect the site from uglier beasts such as the King James Shopping Centre across the road or the destruction which the university wreaked in the elegant terraces of George Square in the 1960s). As David Daiches, one of the city's historians, puts it: the hotel is "so familiar a part of the Edinburgh townscape that like the Scott Monument of 1840-46 it is accepted almost as a natural feature."

Thanks to George Wieland and the North British Railway Company the "monster" was put in precisely the right place to dominate not only the skyline at that end of town, but the social calendar of generations of civic groups. Robert Louis Stevenson called that corner of North Bridge the windiest spot in town, "the high altar in this northern temple of winds". But for anyone arriving by train the NB was the obvious place to stay. For many years anyone entertaining in style had only three choices: North British, Caledonian and The George. And even when the boom of new hotels began in the late 1970s there was still nowhere to compete with the sheer enormity of the banqueting and ball rooms. Indeed, when the hotel's closure for refurbishment coincided with Edinburgh's turn to host the biennial dinner of the Institute of Bankers in Scotland, the Edinburgh bankers were forced to hire a room in Glasgow to feast their guests.

...AND POP STARS STAYED AT THE N.B.
PAUL AND LINDA McCARTNEY

It was the obvious place for the annual dinner and dance for all kinds of people, from the Edinburgh Sir Walter Scott Club who in 1985 drank their 77th toast to the memory of Sir Walter with (Lord) Jo Grimond in the chair and "Longe de Porc Suedoise" on the menu, to the Master Builders Association of Edinburgh and District, who the following year chalked up their 105th annual dinner with a main course of "Roastit ashet O'Bufe wi Wyandour sauce, Ayrshire Tatties an inther Fruits o' the Soil."

When Beatrice Rankin married Scottish golf

champion Alexander Flockart in September 1949 there was no question about the choice for a reception with 300 guests. "It was the obvious place to go," she says, "The rooms were always lovely there. I remember going to the High Constables' and the Dentists' balls for many years." Besides, her father William Rankin, city fruit and flower merchant, had business connections in the old fruitmarket nearby. Staff who worked in the hotel then still remember the display of flowers decorating the dining room and tables for Beatrice's wedding. In a city just beginning to emerge from the gloom of the Second World War the wedding must have been a brilliant splash of colour.

A grand hotel inevitably exists in a social vacuum of its own creation: great events in the outside world may register only as subtle changes in the day's menu. Bob Cunningham, hotel butcher from 1928 until 1959, remembers the disgust of the kitchen staff when boiled tripe appeared on the lunch menu in 1946, a small concession to the post-war austerity reigning beyond the hotel's substantial walls. But a building as big as the NB could not fail to make a mark on the local economy too. In 1913 for example the hotel paid just under £1,000 rates and taxes which included contributions to the police rate, poor rate, water rate and "Inhabited House Duty." Local stores were contracted to supply the formidable inventory of furnishings and fittings and the newly established workshops of the Royal Blind Asylum had regular work manufacturing all kinds of basket ware from linen bins to luncheon hampers. Wages were low — in 1938 Jackie Monteith earned twice as much packing eggs for a farmer as he did cracking them for the head chef at the NB. But the hotel offered a trade, good training and plenty of secure employment: while the Edinburgh Corporation weekly debated the problems of unemployment in the early years of this century, the hotel provided work for 300-400 staff at peak times.

Times change but not always as much as we think. In the 1990s more people live longer and some live better

THE CALCUTTA CUP: THE HOTEL HAS ALWAYS BEEN ASSOCIATED WITH RUGBY

PRIME MINISTER HAROLD WILSON ARRIVES AT THE HOTEL WITH MARY

than they did when the NB first opened. Then Edinburgh people feared tuberculosis; now it is heart disease. The overcrowding and squalor of the old town has changed to a different kind of deprivation among the new housing estates on the outskirts of town, away from the obvious tourist route. When "Butcher" Cunningham started work in the NB kitchen, his home, Corstorphine, was a farming village and he came to the hotel by train. Now the outlying "villages" and "towns" of Leith, Newhaven, Colinton, Corstorphine, are part of the urban sprawl of Edinburgh and people come to work by car (if they can find somewhere to park) or bus. The cable cars which took hotel guests along Princes Street gave way in 1900 to Edinburgh Corporation electric trams in 1926 and trams gave way to buses 30 years later.

But although the city seems a much more congested place the population has remained surprisingly much the same: from 413,008 in 1901 to 433,200 in 1989. The difference is the vast turnover of tourists who now come all year round. By the time the hotel closed in 1988 there were more than two million visitors absorbed by the city that year — 1.27 million from the UK, and just over half a million from overseas. That means four times as many people as the resident population to be housed, fed, entertained and transported.

No wonder new hotels have sprouted at every corner. The newly restored NB with 200 bedrooms still holds the trump card of those enormous function rooms. To the loyal customers of the old days are added the new growing trade of business parties. When the hotel first opened Edinburgh had its own Stock Exchange — now Charlotte Square is an international financial centre attracting business from Japan, America and Europe.

So the social life of Edinburgh has many faces. Great attractions have been added to the city's annual calendar since the first Edinburgh International Festival in 1947 and the first Tattoo in 1968. But different people have always come to the city for different reasons and for many February in Edinburgh means rugby just as to others August means the festival. It also means staying at the North British. Bob Cunningham remembers preparing lamb chops by the hundred for resident rugby followers in the 'fifties. Over 30 years on Jack Maguire remembers persuading Welsh players that they could carrying on drinking all night as long as they stopped singing.

"Forget the festival", says Steve Kew, an oil engineer who travels regularly between London and Aberdeen and tries not to miss a Rugby International. His grandfather always said you could never get a better breakfast than at the North British. "As far as I am concerned Edinburgh means the rugby and the NB. And it always will."

LARGER THAN LIFE

A five star hotel is both a fantasy and a factory. The fantasy is the world the guests enter when they step over the front door. In such a world champagne flows and the patisserie chef can spin spring flowers out of sugar: beds are turned down and lamps lit at bedtime, clean towels appear before each bath, the water is always hot, lifts always work and a boiled egg for breakfast is as perfectly cooked as last night's poached salmon.

"People like to be made to feel at home," says Jack Maguire who spent 40 years in what he describes as a kind of vocation. "They want to be cosseted. They want privacy and they want respect." What people like, head banqueting waiter Renato del Vecchio learned, is to be greeted by someone who knows what they like and exactly how they like it to be done. But whether the rich and famous want to feel at home or homelier bodies want to feel rich and famous — the illusion has to work.

The factory is the extraordinary industry which creates this wonderful world of make-belief from an odd combination of advanced technology, thorough training, and sheer hard work. Breakfast is served for 300 or more because the breakfast chef started worked at 3.30 a.m. Should every guest in the hotel decide to have a bath at the same time water will flow from the hot tap thanks to the chief engineer, his maintenance team and a boiler room which would not have looked out of place in the Queen Mary. Out of sight the waste from guests' plates is compressed by machine and consigned to the deep blue sea. And if the rugby team stays up all night the general manager is thankful that his chief engineer decided to switch over to energy saving lamps.

A hotel is larger than life which means it has all the problems of home many times over. "Imagine a normal house, "says chief engineer Ian Banyard, "then multiply it by 200 and you get some idea of what it takes to run this place." The North British was essentially a self-contained village which until the early 1980s still employed not only a baker, an electrician, a carpenter and a plumber but also a french polisher, an upholsterer and a slater. Ian Banyard reduced the hotel's bill for light bulbs from £7,000 to £5,000 a year by the simple means of buying better quality bulbs, transferring to energy saving lamps and persuading staff to switch off lights when rooms were not in use. He saved £800 a year alone in the huge Sir Walter Scott banqueting room where fifteen chandeliers burned fifteen 60 watt light bulbs each from 6 a.m. until after midnight as breakfast turned into a ceaseless round of catering until the last dinner plate and wine glass gave way to next day's breakfast cups again.

Ian Banyard arrived at the North British in 1983 when the hotel was being wound down for closure and refurbishment. Business continued for five more years with the help of cosmetic redecorations — "a little lipstick here, a little rouge there" as Banyard puts it. But the grand old lady had grown decidedly shabby and beyond the banquets and dinner-dances the veneer of glamour had worn very thin. "The wiring was frayed, the pipe-work was rotten, I was scared to take off the lagging in case the pipes fell to bits."

The boilers which had once pumped steam into the sleeping cars waiting at Platform 19 in the station down below the fourth basement, struggled to meet the demands of bathing guests. Old, outdated and installed in a way which defied access for maintenance, some of the water tanks contained a thick layer of silt which caused a rich, "peaty" flow from the taps when too many baths were run at the same time.

But although the hotel was suffering from years of neglect, the magic was still there largely thanks to the dedication and loyalty of the staff — and by the time the North British clock stopped there were only 60 employees in a building which once gave work for more than 350.

The old place has a powerful effect on most people who work there. "Its ugly but beautiful," says Banyard and other members of staff talk about camaraderie, character and family spirit. Owners have come and gone and there are gaps in the documents and records of the building but the thread of continuity runs in the stories of staff who worked there for years.

Together butcher Bob Cunningham (1929-1954) and sauce chef Jackie Monteith (1938 - 1987) can account for almost 60 years. They recall the heydays before the Second World War when Chef Alfonse Favage ruled the hot and noisy empire of the kitchen, with an insistence on quality and simplicity (just one vegetable or a garnish of cress with grilled meat); a stickler for punctuality and hard work, all argument ceased when he appeared and by his decree rewards were dispensed or withheld. Two bottles of free beer a day for chefs (lem-

FIFTIES STYLE IN THE CAFÉ

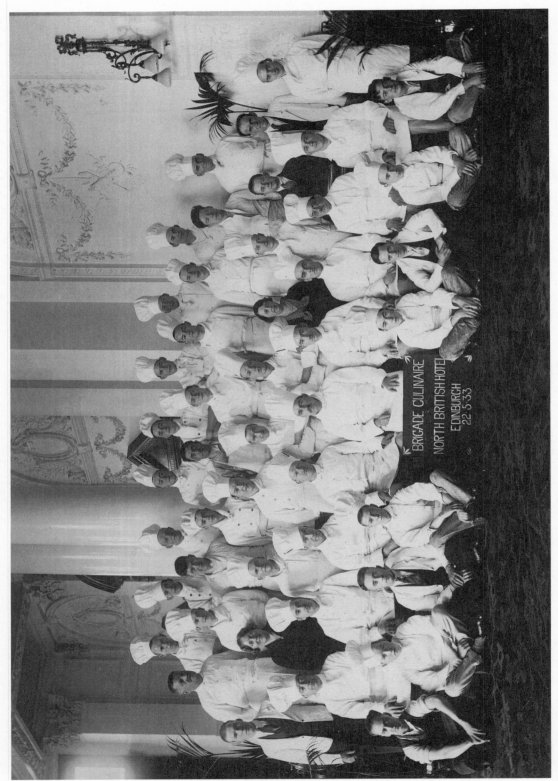

BRIGADE DE CUISINE: MEMBERS OF AN UNDERWORLD WHERE EVERYONE SPEAKS FRENCH.

RENOVATING THE FAMOUS CROWN

onade for apprentices), according to the judgement of M. Favage.

It was a world of bizarre and wonderful contrasts. Pale green damask table clothes decked the restaurant tables and a lunch of roast lamb was around nine shillings — about a week's wage for a young trainee chef as Monteith remembers without resentment. Guests sat down to choose from a menu offering perhaps "potage aux huitres" followed by "grouse en chaudfroid" unaware that just beneath this oasis of quiet luxury was the mezzanine floor of the kitchen, an oddly international underworld where apprentices wheeled out waste by the barrow, former prisoners from Saughton scrubbed and spread sawdust on the floor, and everyone spoke French. Scots like Cunningham and Monteith struggled to learn the foreign language of cuisine and so did the young Italian Renato del Vecchio when he joined as commis waiter in 1969 with barely a word of English.

Bob Cunningham still possesses a photograph of the huge "Brigade Culinaire", taken in 1933, which shows a strictly ordered society, with M. Favage fixed firmly in the centre. It had not changed much when Jackie Monteith started as an apprentice making today's tartare sauce from yesterday's mayonnaise and wearing a borrowed white coat because he couldn't afford to buy one out of his week's wage of 7s 6d. He thought he would not stay longer than the first week. "I had never heard so much shouting." But the excitement of the place grew on him, he discovered a leaning for the work, he enjoyed the artistry involved in creating the fantasy. Most of all he like the camaraderie and bustle in the kitchen. "It was busy, busy, busy — like King's Cross Station."

What all the staff remember with pride is the training provided by the North British, a legacy from the old railway company which was to be handed on by the nationalised transport hotel group. Head waiters, chefs and managers have pursued careers across the world on the strength of a North British training. Helga de Bordes, now returned to Austria, kept notes from her 1933 training course at the hotel, which instructed staff in the art of recognising different types of patrons. The social order is set out thus: "(a) business man, (b) business woman, (c) old people, (d) children. (e) irritable person, (f) guest who tries to be too personal, (g) timid person, (h) leisure class type."

The links with the railway were severed in the early 1980s — not a happy decade for the hotel as its ownership changed rapidly in an extended game of company takeovers. The start of the 1990s, however, brought again the prospect of a settled future under the ownership of a company with a similar vision of the hotel and its place to that created by its founders at the start of the century. Balmoral International Hotels, a new company based in Edinburgh, bought the North British with the intention of making it a flagship for an international hotel group with luxury hotels in strategic cities in the United Kingdom, Europe and North America. It is an ambition of which the directors of the North British Railway Company would have approved.

History has an odd way of repeating itself. The new Edinburgh Balmoral has a style and appearance very close to the spirit of the building which took its triumphant place on the Edinburgh skyline as the century began — indeed it deliberately evokes the Edwardian era which has become a symbol of timeless comfort and security the world over: tea may be taken in the Palm Court whatever is happening in the real world outside. Very deeply rooted in local history the Edinburgh Balmoral will compete with the best of hotels anywhere in the world just as George Wieland intended when he led the "Waverley Station Hotel Committee" on a grand tour across Europe all those years ago. The name may have changed but the sense of identity has turned full circle.

THE REFURBISHMENT BEGINS

106

SHROUDED IN SCAFFOLDING.

INDEX OF ADVERTISERS

By Appointment to
Her Majesty The Queen
Silversmiths and Clock Specialists

HAMILTON & INCHES

L I M I T E D

Gold and
Silversmiths,
Jewellers, Watch
and Clockmakers
FOUNDED 1866

87 George Street,
Edinburgh
EH2 3EY
TELEPHONE
031 225 4898

"Reverie"

Since 1866 we have been purveyors of beautiful Jewels, Silver
and Objects of the highest quality for the one you adore.

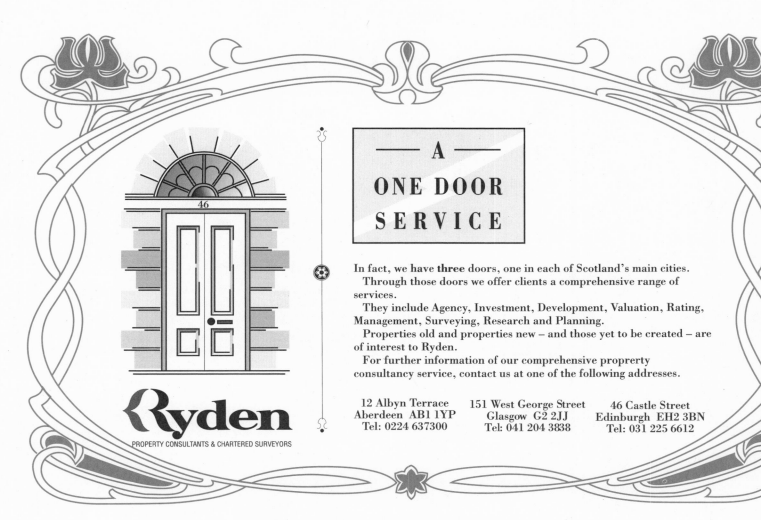

III

The Walkers Bakery Shop in High Street, Aberlour. Opening Hours: 7.00a.m.-5.00p.m.

WALKERS SHORTBREAD

BAKERS OF PURE BUTTER SHORTBREAD

A TRADITION OF QUALITY
SINCE 1898

Made to the Original Highland Recipe.
Using Only The Finest Ingredients Possible To Obtain.

Walkers
Shortbread
Aberlour, Strathspey
Scotland.

MAINTAINING EDINBURGH'S INTERNATIONAL SPIRIT

Sir Harry Lauder

Mons Meg

Eric Liddle

THAT SCOTTISH LIQUEUR

Greyfriars Bobby

Edinburgh Castle

Robert Louis Stevenson

 GLAYVA LIQUEUR LTD. SPONSORS OF THE EDINBURGH MILITARY TATTOO

FROM INVERGORDON DISTILLERS GROUP

VII

WALFORDS

CONSTRUCTION CONSULTANTS

and

CHARTERED QUANTITY SURVEYORS

PROVIDING AN OVERALL COST ADVICE

SERVICE

FOR THE NORTH BRITISH HOTEL

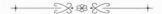

IN 1990 WALFORDS ARE ACTIVELY

INVOLVED IN PROJECTS THROUGHT

THE U.K., MAINLAND EUROPE AND

NORTH AFRICA

CONTACT US IN EDINBURGH AT

26 ALVA STREET, EDINBURGH

TEL: 031 226 2791

LONDON • LIVERPOOL • LUTON • MANCHESTER • HORSHAM

Justerini & Brooks

Justerini & Brooks have been wine merchants since 1749. During that time our fine wines cognacs spirits liqueurs and vermouths have been found on the dining tables of the most discerning private houses and restaurants throughout the Kingdom. We are proud to continue that tradition and carry the most comprehensive stock of wines from all over the world.

Amongst the spirits that we carry we have a selection of over one hundred and thirty malt whiskies from which to choose.

We look forward to welcoming you to our elegant shops at 39 George Street, Edinburgh and at 61 St James's Street, London.

SCOTCH **J&B** WHISKY

RARE

J & B Rare Scotch Whisky is a top quality, highly distinctive and stylish brand of blended Scotch Whisky – distinctive particularly for its superior smoothness and natural pale colour – it is indeed a wine merchants whisky.

J & B RARE – Uncommonly good Scotch Whisky

J & B also produce a very fine single malt – Knockando and a deluxe whisky – 15 year old J & B Reserve.

J & B Rare is sold all over the world and has been awarded the Queens award for Export Achievement on five occasions.

THE QUEENS AWARD FOR
EXPORT ACHIEVEMENT
1 9 8 5

THE QUEENS AWARD FOR
EXPORT ACHIEVEMENT
1 9 8 9

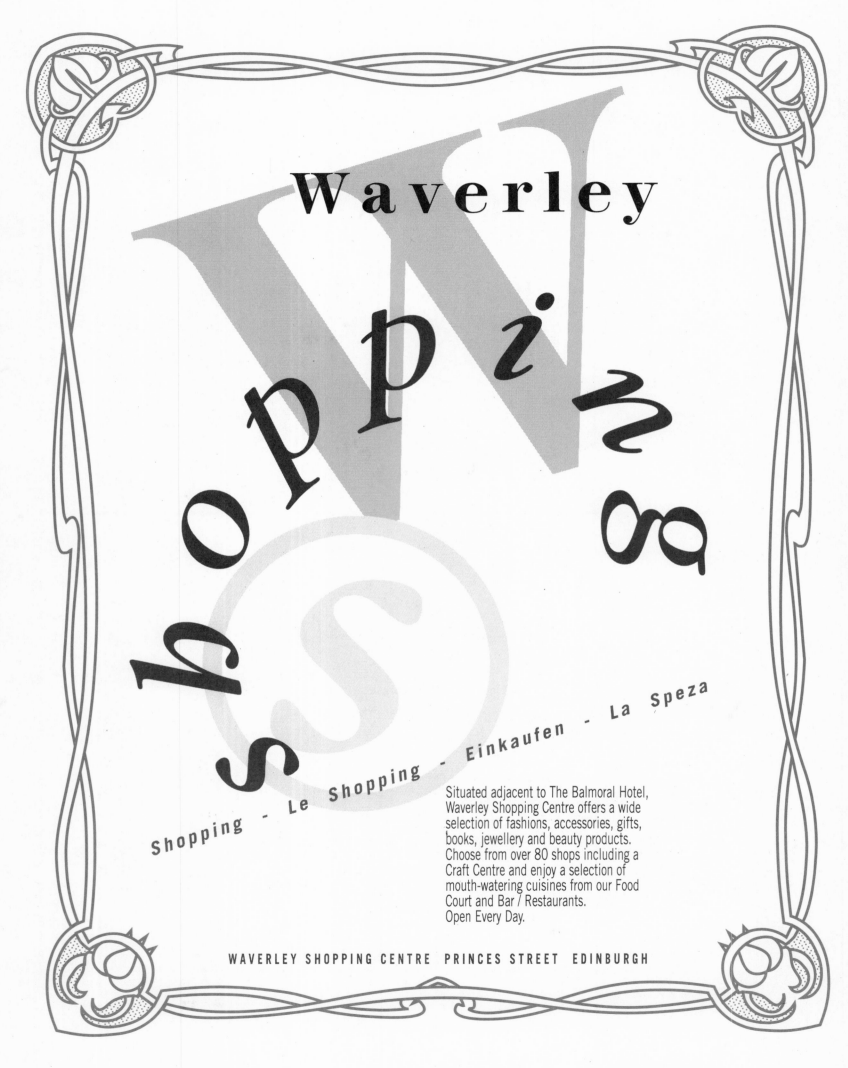

Waverley

Shopping

Shopping - Le Shopping - Einkaufen - La Speza

Situated adjacent to The Balmoral Hotel, Waverley Shopping Centre offers a wide selection of fashions, accessories, gifts, books, jewellery and beauty products. Choose from over 80 shops including a Craft Centre and enjoy a selection of mouth-watering cuisines from our Food Court and Bar / Restaurants. Open Every Day.

WAVERLEY SHOPPING CENTRE   PRINCES STREET   EDINBURGH

BOLLINGER

Champagne